A MAN LIKE ME

Noteography Of A Father To His Son

'Debayo Coker

A MAN LIKE ME

Noteography of A Father To His Son

Copyright© 2014 'Debayo Coker

All rights reserved.

No part of this book may be used or reproduced by any means, graphic, electronic, or mechanical, including photocopying, recording or taping or by any information retrieval system without the written permission of the publisher except in the case of brief quotations embodied in critical articles and reviews.

This is a work of fiction. All of the characters, names, incidents, organizations, and dialogue in this novel are either the products of the author's imagination or are used fictitiously.

First published in the USA, April, 2014.

Published in Nigeria by
Beeni Global Resources
381, Borno Way,
Yaba,
Lagos, Nigeria.
PO Box 3405, Somolu,
Lagos, Nigeria.
Tel: +2348033225953/+2349096991619
beeniglobalresources@gmail.com
www.debayocoker.com

ISBN: 978-978-941-591-5

Printed in the United States of America.

DEDICATION

To...

My father.

My son.

Every responsible father.

And to every woman playing the role of a father.

THE COMMUNITY: PREFACE	1
HE KNEW YOU: THE PROLOGUE	3
CREDENDUM TO MY SON	8
NOW YOU HAVE A NAME	16
COME HERE SON: THE FUNDAMENTALS	21
OUR CODES	26
LET'S FILL THIS FORM	35
YOUR EDUCATOR	39
CLEAR THE PASSAGEWAYS	44
WHAT IS THIS, SON?	46
WE HAVE A TASK	48
AUNTY KORE	52
WHAT! FUNDAMENTALS CONTINUE	58
ODD VENUES	63
YO MOMMA!	66
NOT YOUR FAULT	69
WHY I DON'T HAVE BENTLEY.	72
LET'S TALK: FAST LANE	74
ON YOUR OWN	82

YOU ARE MY SON	86
WE HAVE A GIRL	91
FISHING	98
CRACK KNUCKLE	103
OF HAPPINESS, OF RICHES, OF WEALTH	106
BEYOND TIME	109
GET FIRED	111
WHILE 'U WAIT	117
I SAW HER	120
NEV'LAND	123
PECULIAR	126
POLITICS	130
SEAFARER: NAVAL OFFICER	134
THAT IS MY SON	136
STEER THE WHEEL	138
HONESTLY, I DON'T KNOW	140
DISCUSSION CONTINUES...	143
WHY I DID IT: THE EPILOGUE	146
BACK TO SCHOOL: ABOUT THE AUTHOR	

THE COMMUNITY: PREFACE

𝒟ear family members and friends,

How is your day going at your different ends? I have not been able to watch the cable network for international news lately but I want to believe there is nothing unpalatable happening at your end.

I have been dynamically transfixed in a literary exercise, held bound, to the scripting of this compendium of notes as all events in here are anticipatory. My adrenaline flight just touched down and I look somewhat satisfied by the voyage whose experience I want to share with you.

Kindly take a time out to grasp these momenta when you are most relaxed in body, soul and spirit in order to ably welcome the pointrel that will come to work on your heart as it is inherent in this life sojourn. Expressly, literary, academically, socially and what have you, whatsoever point of view you look at it from just don't lose the foci herein.

I hope you will be far better off than you were before you embarked on this trip with me.

Our utmost solace will come when we, together, excel in discharging our duties and performing the responsibilities that we all have as a community of people.

"Train up a child the way he should go and when he is old he will not depart from it." Prov. 22:6.

I love you all.

'Debayo Coker

HE KNEW YOU: THE PROLOGUE

Dear son,

Long before you were formed in your mother's womb God knew you. He is the one that has committed you into my care and Him I am accountable to regarding anything that may happen to you while you will be under my care. So we will both be working together to achieve the vision of God for our lives.

I must let you know that I will be bringing you up through my life's experiences. I am not at all a perfect person as you will find out that this book does not cover all issues of fatherhood in relationship with son-hood as many are the varied issues being experienced in different homes all over the world but, know that I did my best to treat every topic that came to my mind as at the time of compiling these notes and that is why I am praying that God gives me the grace to remember where I had fallen and inform you so that you won't stumble at that spot as I believe the stump is still there. You deserve a smooth ride and this you can enjoy to the fullest by learning from the experiences of others that have gone ahead of you and have trodden the paths that you may want to go.

MyPD and I have prepared ourselves to receive you as adequate provision has been made for you to the end that we are blessed by God.

I watched MyPD as she carried you in her womb wishing I could look through her tummy and see what you are looking like but patience as a virtue is required for the full cycle to be completed. You should be here anytime soon as you are knocking at the door already.

I have tried my best reading through all the books that I can lay my hands on that address the topic of fatherhood but there is something that I really want to know which is the communication avenue that could be explored to promote the relationship between a father and his son, as communication is needed to achieve a set goal especially when we will be working together as a team.

I came across two great books in my research which I found more interesting than others. They bequeath timeless pieces of wisdom to humankind. The book of Proverbs in the bible and secondly The Prince by Nichollo Machiavelli are unquantifiable, in my judgment, as regards fatherhood and parenting.

King Solomon as a father wrote those Proverbs to his son while Machiavelli wrote his treatise to a prince who had lost his father.

This compendium of notes is my gift to you my Son.

I stood close to the window looking into the celestial horizon, racking my brain on how I will continue working on a script I got stuck writing, then my adrenaline flight took me to write out a message through which I intend to announce your birth on some social media platforms so I wrote out CREDENDUM TO MY SON first, but the flow would not stop, so, I decided to make a collection of projectorial notes of certain and likely events that will and likely happen as we come to bond together.

Please, when you will be reading these notes, make sure you open your mind to understand the loaded meaning the strings of words connote, not just on the peripheral.

You can best understand these notes if you string them as a whole; but reading them in isolation and randomly will not depreciate their signification. Mostly, they are referential, one to another, anaphorically as well as cataphorically.

I am in by no way demanding that you conform yourself to the events that are recorded in the noteography as self-discovery is very unique a journey that everyone needs to tread on his or her own. Pick the ones that may work for you and concoct them with what you may have discovered as unique to your situations. I pray the good God leads your path.

For the people that I could or could not mention in the course of this book due to space, I want you to know that you are still part of the community and we all have higher responsibilities in ensuring that our wards are brought up in accordance with good values.

I must say a very big thank you to my parents for giving me the avenue to come through to the world.

I love you all my siblings as we are co-travelers along the same path to the world.

I lean on friends for balance as I careen through this world. I cannot thank you enough.

My teachers shaped me to becoming a man of good morals. Thank you for consolidating on what my parents did.

MyPD tolerates my excesses and accepts my shortfalls. Rarely are there women that could manage a writer. She understandably adapts to my impulsive artistic demand for solitariness. She lives in my heart.

God Almighty, the giver of all gifts, you so bless me by establishing me as a nation. Forever I will worship you.

Everyone needs a father or a father figure but ultimately God is the Father of everyone.

I love you my son.

'Debayo Coker

CREDENDUM TO MY SON

Welcome to the world.

You arrived on Thursday, the 17th of April, 2014, the same day my father clocked 64 years old. We would have been celebrating my mother's 63rd birthday in a week's time if she had been alive. It is a blessing we will be christening you on her birthday.

I strongly believe you had a jolly ride here. I could tell from your springy activities even in your mother's womb as we listened to your heartbeat during the many routine scans we had.

You were so lively a fetus long before the medicals could determine some other things. There was a day they wanted to confirm your gender; funnily, you crossed your legs so they could not tell. You pranked us all for weeks.

I watched as your mother carried you in her womb for those 38 weeks. Son, she is a very strong woman to bear that load for that gestation period. Sometimes I wish I could relieve her of the burden of carrying the protruding belly all around but I am not anatomically programmed for that.

I watched as she practically nurtured you in her womb through many sleepless nights. Early morning rise just to keep up with ante-natal appointments. On many occasions she had to jettison her own business appointments just to make sure she took you to the doc.

Son, you sure need to see the ante partum and parturition pictures of your mother. Each time, I look at those pictures my respect for her and my mother increases. Mothers deserve our gratitude always. Honor, respect, and adore your mother always. They gave us life.

As I hold you in my arms I see a split image of myself. No doubt, you are fearfully and wonderfully created in the image and in the likeness of God but you are my reflection and I am your mirror. I see myself through you as you will be looking up to me.

It is a task that we both must work to achieve.

We share the same story. I grew up to know my grandfather. Your grandfather may walk in any moment from now. My mother was a very positive influence on me, I wish you had met her but don't worry I will teach you all she taught me. And boy you are so blessed I am around likewise your mother so you will get a bumper package for I know your mother is loaded with goodies that you will enjoy for a very long time as she will not die in a very long time to come just as myself. So be prepared for double barrels of good parenting.

You will be growing up seeing and talking to your father every day. Sometimes I may not be there with you physically due to some other commitments, I sure will not deny you my voice through the phone, every day, no matter what the other commitments may be. I won't raise my voice at you not to talk of my hand but know that you will be adequately reprimanded for any act of juvenile cheekiness. I don't want you to grow up cursing your father for indulging you in anyway.

Let me make this promise to you, I WILL NEVER INDULGE YOU NOT TO TALK OF OVER-INDULGENCE.

I won't throw any chair in this house or any other house as not to put you in any state of confusion by providing an alibi for your friends and classmates as to why your father would do such a thing. No public disgrace I mean. I will only exact my pugilistic fervidness on anything that may want to separate us. Boy, you will be my best friend.

There is a legacy that I will love you to pursue. It will be fruitless writing this note to you if you have not even followed that legacy. In anything, you MUST get education my son. That is the only accoutrement you will need to fight the wintry grip of ignorance. It is so essential you do this as to break any veil off your eyes that many situations may want to harass you with. Even the Lord Jesus admonished us to always seek the truth. There is a book that you MUST also read alongside any other book: It is called The Bible. It points you to the right direction. It is full of knowledge. You will be richly blessed reading this Book of Life. Your mother and I have studied it and all the principles we will be guiding you with are from inside of it. We have even bought you a copy.

Humanity is so sweet. Loving, respecting and treating everyone with kindness are so very important to maintain that cord that binds us all.

DO NOT treat anyone with sniffy separatism.

DO NOT be kind to a man that is adorned with gold and be rash to a man that is seemingly appearing like a pauper. What a man wears does not necessarily define him. Deal with people equally regardless of class and status. What is good for the goose is also good for the gander.

Before I pass something over, you MUST also know when to stand and fight for your rights.

This is so important because people will attempt to fill you with gall. There are many predators out there, Son. Reject any act of contempt meted to you meticulously. I am sure you will never bow to any form of roughneckism. Stand and defend yourself. You are a MAN.

In all, be fair to your conscience.

MyPD could not stop telling the story of how her father would come pick her from school, bare her on his shoulders and talked with her as they walked back to his office where he would leave his car. I loved that act and since your maternal granddad is no more around to do that for you I will be helping him out. I will come to pick you in the school ANYTIME I AM AVAILABLE, bear you on my shoulders and we will walk a long distance together as we talk so as to allow you share your school experience with me. Hey, you will be getting a cone of ice cream each time I come.

I know you will want to fly. I won't clip your wings but will check all excesses. I am a wordsmith, a passionate arts enthusiast. I know you know that so well. But if you want to follow Einsteinian path you are so welcome. If it is Fordic journey you will want to tread, so many more grounds to break. You will grow to your utmost possibility. As long as you will want to dream and explore them you are most welcome Son. Don't let me forget to add, I have some classical songs that you may like as you may want to tow the step of Nightingale and some books that may engrave Shakespearian exploits on your heart. Whatever career path you choose I am here for you. But know wildness is not a way of life. You MUST NOT go that way.

Before I round up this note to you, I want to let you know I witnessed my grandfather's interment. My father was so ripened in age while he buried his own father. I was by his side. My father is still alive. In essence, what I am saying is, do not be in a hurry to leave this stage. I will bury my father when he finally passes. And you will bury me when I finally pass in my very old age. I will never witness your departure. You are a gift from God to me and the gift of God is without repentance. Since God will not take you away from me NOTHING in the world will prevail and take you away from me. You will live to fulfill the goodness of the Lord in the land of the living. You will be great.

Whatever the achievements of my father were, I dwarfed them in my twenties. Everything. Whatever achievements I may record in my lifetime, Son, you will dwarf them in your teen.

You will be greater than me. You will be greater than your forebears. The earth will open and yield its increase onto you.

You have been knighted into glory through the blood of Jesus Christ and no adversity will be able to hold you down in Jesus name.

Where my father fell I learnt from and whatever mistakes I may have made will not count against you. No force, of whatever background, will have power over you in Jesus name.

Help shall come from all the points of the world to favor you. Men will go out of their ways to do your bidding. Kings will seek you and bless you. Man of wisdom and knowledge of God shall you grow to be. You will impact your generation so positively. You have been called out of darkness into light, the light of God will not depart your life.

You are blessed and highly favored.

Papyrus is long obsolete. Paper may soon go into extinction. But these platforms are what I strongly foresee that your generation will get to use that is why I chose to communicate to you via these medium, that is to tell you that I am moving ahead of time.

I hope this note finds you in abundant joy my son. I love you always.

Your father,

'Debayo Coker

NOW YOU HAVE A NAME

Son, traditionally, where I come from, a child is named on the eighth day of his birth. The faith that I hold in high esteem, Christianity, also supports the custom that christening be done on the eighth day of a child's birth. Hence you are just being christened today.

I owe you every obligation to explain the meaning of the names that I call you and the reason(s) why I chose those names.

ILE LAA WO KATO SO OMO L'ORUKO is a saying in my place that translates to mean autochthonal circumstances determine the name given to a child.

Long before now, nativism was just the only consideration in naming a child but the advent of colonialism brought so much change to our worldview, especially when a child's name must be anglicized or totally re-christened an English name by his/her parents or the teachers for him/her to access education during that period. Now it has become a norm for a child to have an English or Christian name as they call it. You ask who the colonialists are. Well, son, you have a lot to learn, so we will take it one at a time. That is a topic for another day.

The other day, long before I had you, I decided to travel to a neighboring state, Ibadan to be precise. I went with a public transport and at the park a vendor who introduced himself as Samson and boasted so much of having conducted a wide research on names advertised his compendium of names and their meanings.

He said there are some names he would never call his child. He mentioned David and Solomon amongst many but those two, I remember so vividly. He said the former was a killer and the latter lost his kingdom at the end of his reign. Anyway, he is entitled to his opinion. But Son I will encourage you to read about this duo in the bible, you would see the great exploits they did and the immensity of God's love and grace upon their lives; their records are peerless even till date. If you look at the flag of Israel you will see a hexagram figure in there, it is known as the Star of David; and the promises of God to Solomon still stand till date that no one will ever beat that record in this world.

Also about Samson to see the antitheses in the lives of some people and you will wonder why the vendor has not effected a change of name.

A piece of advice son, whenever you hear someone speak in public and you find such to be blasphemous, please never join issue(s) with such as foolishness and bigotry are attendant results of ignorance.

Just as I mentioned earlier, names are usually given circumstantially. Read the stories of Jabez and Ichabod in the bible. There are some names as well that people will refrain from giving their child due to the nefariousness nature of a bearer of such a name, e.g., Anini. Am sure google will be so much instrumental if you want to read about his life.

Now let me tell you why I called you those names of yours.

Alexander means a helper of men. I studied the chivalry of great men of old: they were brave men; prowess and conquest were forms of great achievements. To tell you the truth, Son, you will marvel at the exploits of such men when you study them. You will live long, full of wisdom and people will seek the good counsel you are full of. I will let you know more reasons I chose this name subsequently.

Adesiremi. This is another of your names. You were given this name for a particular reason. Several months before I had you, I was in a state of confusion as I had no means to provide for your mother and I. No job or business. Everything crumbled. But thank God for His mercies as He opened my eyes to see His goodness again few months before you came. That is, you came at the point of my breakthrough. You can see it is a name well chosen. Circumstantialism in a child's naming. Remember?

Oluwalonimi. Am sure you wonder why this one again. I will tell you its meaning then you will appreciate the magnitude of God. Though I am your earthly father but there is a Father that is beyond all fathers that even I, your earthly father run to Him for my supplies. He created everything, without Him nothing is created. He owns you, your mother and I. Everything. So this name means God owns me.

Petrus. This is a German variation of Peter the rock. Peter was one of the disciples of Jesus. This name was given to you by your godmother, Ms. Christine Wong. She is German. She gave you this name long before the bed of our copulation that led to your conception was laid. I will show you her pictures and possibly you will get to meet her someday. She lives in Bad Durcheim, Mannheim, Germany.

As you can see that you have many names. So is the tradition and culture we have here. But I have chosen to call you the following.

Remember I told you I will tell you more reason I like that name Alexander. MyPD smiles at the hearing of that name, invariably she chose it for you as she even likes the female variance, Alexandra in case she gave birth to a female.

Here is more reason I chose those names:

Al-Desiremi Adebayo-Coker.

Aesthetically, what do you see?

I took the Al from Alexander and joined it with Desiremi from Adesiremi. Adebayo-Coker is a compound name formation of both my first and last names. These two will form your own surname. I hope you absolve it all now.

If anyone asks you: what is your name?

Answer: AL-DESIREMI ADEBAYO-COKER.

You are blessed and highly favored my son.

I love you my son.

'Debayo Coker

COME HERE SON: THE FUNDAMENTALS

𝒟ear Son,

Barely have I finished praying for you this morning that I have pressing issues on my heart that I must expressly discuss with you. I know you may not be able to talk to me because you are just few days old but I know if you could leap, hearing my voice in your mother's womb, then you can hear me now.

I have to impress these fundamentals on your heart so that they be part of you. Most important are my blessings on you and so are these maxims that I want to share with you.

There is just one GOD my son. He is the Almighty. He is The Omnipotent and The Omniscient. Everything comes from Him. Outside of Him there is nothing. Before you were formed in your mother's womb, He knew you. Long before the creation of this world He had you in His plan. Even before I write this note to you He knew on this date at this time I will write it even before I myself was born or even my forebears. Am sure you may be wondering who this God is? As you look into my eyes you will see Him there. As you look at your mother He is with her. As you grow to become a man He is with you. He is so powerful and so kind. If He were not kind, son, as you will get to learn more about Him, you will see that nothing should have been left to live. You MUST strive to learn about and love Him with the whole of your heart at all times.

To know this God you MUST study the bible. Son, I am telling you about Him not because I want you to be a Christian like myself and my forebears but because He is The Way, The Light and The Life. If you have Him there is nothing that will shake you in this world. Remember your name, OLUWALONIMI, He owns you.

Do you know another thing that I want you to know about this God? He can be communicated to directly without any intermediary. Awesome you say? Yes. With His so much power you don't need to go through anyone to reach Him, just as you have an open access to me anytime and even when I am going to be away from home at times as occasion may demand you can still reach me on the phone. But one thing about Him is that He is not away at any time and He hears you always. He doesn't sleep nor slumber; He is unlike myself that may fall asleep or become absent minded while you talk with me. He is always with you and at hand to attend to you anytime. All you need to do is to pray to Him. As you will see that for some days that you have been with us we-your mother, I and even you wake up each morning, kneel down to say some words. That is an act of praying. Don't worry you will get to know Him more and how to reach Him. Son, He is good.

As you can hear us this morning after the Morning Prayer the first words your mother and I shared were GOOD MORNING MyPD.

Son, culturally, a son will go to his parents in the morning, prostrate himself and say Good Morning sir/ma. That act gladdens the hearts of his parents and they unleash blessings upon him. Those prayers by parents go a long way to mold the life of the child. And that is what we put to practice, every morning, when we receive the grace to wake up in the morning; we kneel down and pray to God. It is a way of saying Good Morning and Thank you our Father.

Another thing that I want you to know is that I watched you few days ago while your mother breast fed you. You seemed to have bitten her breast. Though you have not grown any teeth but you did it with your gum. Smilingly, you looked at her as she screamed. Funny boy you are. Son, I want you to know that woman is my wife before she is your mother and any act of unfeelingness to her by ANYBODY will bring coldness between myself and the person, whosoever. I can never grow cold towards you hence I am letting you know not to bite my wife because if I let it pass without caution you will do it when you are denticulate.

And son, this one is also important. Though I know you can't voice your gratitude as of now but please learn to smile just as you are smiling now for every act of kindness done to you. Do you know that that Almighty God that I told you about earlier also revels in our thank-youliness? As your mother breast feed you, smile at her. Son, am sure she will gladly breast feed you even when you are not hungry. Fine, it is your right but to unlock your access to some things or even get more than you deserve as your rights, your expression of gratitude is so cogent. I will start paying your school fees, it is my responsibility to do that and you're right it is to get good education but when you say DAD, THANK YOU FOR PAYING MY SCHOOL FEES that will propel me to pay your school fees in advance. Do you get it?

People will give you gifts as you will get to see. No matter what they give you, as long as it is not what you bought with your own money, son, learn to say thank you. Even if it is what you buy with your money say thank you for the delivery. MyPD will be serving you food in time, learn to say thank you Mommy. If you do that you get a bigger chunk subsequently.

Am sure you will wonder why I call my wife and she calls me MyPD? I will tell you in a subsequent note: OUR CODES.

More fundamentals will follow as you get to understand things the more.

Love you son.

'Debayo Coker

OUR CODES

𝒟ear Son,

You are wondering why I have to let the public consume what I call codes. Expectedly, your observation is welcome. But take a seat. I assure you no one will know our codes. They are too codified to be demystified by anyone. Winks>

Let me start by telling you what codes are. I am copying from the WordWeb application that I have on my laptop as the definitions that are provided here are at par with those I have in mind. A code is a set of rules, principles or laws (especially written ones). A coding system is used for transmitting messages requiring brevity or secrecy.

Additionally, a code is a language that is shared by a caucus/society/people, etc. Codes appear mystic to those that are outside of the sect but so usual to those that is therein.

Hope my own definition is not confusing? Let me explain.

I had to learn Deutsch (German) in order to communicate effectively with Ms. Wong, Dein

Patentante (Your godmother). So you can see that language too is a code. English, German, Chinese, French, etc. are all forms of codes but they have been thrown open to the world so anyone so interested could learn the language if he/she is not a primary speaker. A primary speaker of a language is that person that has all innate abilities to pick the language as a result of birth, parental link, etc.

You wonder why the world is striving towards different language acquisitions. Well I could only answer that in relation to the economic value and importance a language has come to attain. Remember, I have to learn German to communicate effectively with Ms. Wong. And if you remember as part of the Fundamentals that I talked to you about, a Christian is expected to pray in order to communicate effectively with God. That is a code son because there are things one should know before one could communicate EFFECTIVELY with God. Don't worry you will learn them. We go one step at a time.

I was a student of English language, and one of the courses so interesting to me was Social Discourse. It is a field in Linguistic studies. I will urge you to observe people when they talk; no one is alienated from his environment, culture, religion, education, profession, etc. in a communication exchange with another person.

There was a President that went to visit an American President. During their conversation the host spoke with him looking directly into his eyes while he tried as much as possible to evade the stare. Some people berated him for such evasion but I made some people that I could talk to understand that he was justified in doing that because where he came from you don't look into peoples' eyes while talking to them especially when they are older or more powerful than you are. It will be taken as tantamount to disrespect. Whereas, in the host's culture if you evade eye contact with your communicator it will be taken that you're full of lies. So you see what coding is like.

Tone, Pitch, Facial expression, Body language, etc. play roles in information dissemination and interpretation. Hope I have told you the whole essence of coding is for information dissemination and interpretation? There is a lot to learn. Son!

Let me tell you a story.

Precisely in 1986, but I could not remember the exact month. I was barely Six years old. I went with my mother to her friend's house. It was much later that I understood what transpired. My mother hadn't seen this classmate of hers in a very long time and they were kind of reuniting after few years of separation. I was gaily dressed looking sharp and prim. My mother had to take me to the barber herself that morning and I was given a smart parting to the left side of my head, son that was the rave of the moment at that time, just as Mo Hawk, and other haircuts that you guys have now.

We got to the friend's house somewhere in Ikoyi as my mother's friend was married to a high class businessman-cum-politician at that time. We were living in Bariga and my father was a storekeeper with a blue chip company. Anyways, I was met with serene ambience and nicely scented atmosphere welcomed by a well-dressed concierge. I was swept off my feet, Son.

My mother and her friend greeted one another and settled to catching up. While they were doing their chatting I watched as the chef set the table with arrays of cuisines. I was agape with wonderment at the various dishes adorning the table. Son that was the first time I will be seeing such. Do not blame me son as I know your own code is different.

My mother had to answer for me when I was asked my name as my eyes were transfixed on the table still. Each time that scene comes to mind, I smile at my gross innocence.

Truly I had a good meal that day but I later regretted for having to eat the food at all. You would not want to know what happened to me afterwards.

I got home that day and my mother reported the case to my father, Daddy mi as we codified him: A No- nonsense -man. Son, your grandfather used to be very active. He beat the hell out of me without even considering my innocence. I learnt the hard way.

I don't want you to learn the hard way my son. So let me tell you some codes.

Culturally, as a sign of respect, when you see an elderly person, man or woman, you MUST greet them by prostrating and even if you stand up and they offer to shake you, you MUST receive their handshake so warmly with your right hand and with a bow.

Take note, you must wait for them to offer their arms to you in a handshake not you offering yours first. At times, you may want to prostrate and some elders will stop you by offering out their arms for a handshake, receive the handshake by bowing your head. You will say ' Did you say bow?' Yes, that is what I said. You will ask but God said we should not bow to anyone/god but Him. Son, I like that curiosity. The kind of bow here is not in their worship but a sign of respect that you must accord to people older than you. Get it.

Another thing you must know is that in a conversation with anybody, never interrupt them while they are talking regardless of their age, color, education, religion, etc.; though MyPD may not totally agree with this because she is a lawyer; you will understand how those guys called lawyers talk. (LOL)

Back to our flow; do not interrupt people while they are talking. Just listen to them air their views then you can now respond. Do you know why I asked you to listen first? Well, so that you can make the rightful judgment as to whether their conversation is worth listening or responding to. You should not waste your energy on futile talks.

In dealing with people, even with myself, there is a high tendency of friction occurrence. I will urge you to study Crises Management; it is a phenomenal part of People Management from which you cannot escape as long as you remain on this earth because oftentimes, you will come in contact with people everywhere you go. Being armed with this skill will go a long way in helping you engage in good communication.

People are of different backgrounds. Populi Majeure. In some of your interaction with other humans, you will discover that they are bound to be hurt because of what you say or do. Some of them will approach you to tell you that you hurt them with your words or acts and some of them may quietly react to your utterance(s) or action(s).

Son, whichever way, anytime you discover or you are approached that you have hurt anyone by your words and actions, learn to say 'I am sorry'. Say it and mean it. Do you know why? It makes you a stronger and better person. Do not hold grudges against anyone. Live in peace with every person. Remember I told you in my first note to you that you must be fair to your conscience at all times.

I do not want to make this particular note too long for you so that you can digest the information herein intended. Let me quickly talk about one more subject here and to fulfill my promise to you on why I codified your mother MyPD.

After my father beat me that day, I have learnt to control my appetite and also refine my nuisance. Do you know how? I have learnt to ignore food even in my own house. There are three things that are commonly known to bring man to a fall so easily - money, women and food.

Let us talk about food now, the other two you will sure learn about in later times. I will share my experience on them in subsequent notes.

Food in this sense consists of anything that you put into your mouth that you eat and swallow down your tummy, water, juice, yoghurt, etc. all fall within this categorization. I want you to study the story of Daniel in the bible; you will find him so interesting.

I know you will feel hunger; for goodness sake you are human. But learn to ignore the feeling AT TIMES. If you do that you will see that even if you go to a place and you are presented with a great table of different assortments of food, you won't betray yourself and I.

There are some inner codes that I am going to teach you- some facial, body and eye contacts systemization so that you will know some things, like who to greet and how to greet, when to greet a person or to eat at a place. It is our coded code.

Now let me tell you why I call my wife, your mother MyPD.

It is a love code. Wondering what is love? You will know about it in time but know above all that God loves you even more than I love you.

My Precious Diamond-MyPD that is the decipherment of the code. It is one in a multitude. If you hear any other person use that code, then he or she has stolen or copied it from us.

Another important code you must know is that whenever you want to enter a place, no matter where it is, you must learn to knock on the door if it is not left opened.

You walked up on MyPD and I the other day, without knocking on the door. What you saw us doing was an activity solely for wife and husband.

We will come back to talk more about it in time.

I love you dear son.

'Debayo Coker

LET'S FILL THIS FORM

𝒟ear Son,

"Come let us reason together" so says part of a verse in the book of Isaiah.

I saw that there were some things that you did not understand while we were filling your elementary school entrance form.

There are some privileges that one consanguineously enjoy by being born into a family. MyPD, yourself and myself make up a family. I have brothers and sisters, so does MyPD. You will get to have brothers and sisters too.

No one is an isolated man. We are all part of a nucleus that in turn forms part of a whole. We all are linked on the society level; as you can see that we have neighbors who are people living around us. They share the same properties in relation to their families and somehow to us by living together with us in this community. I will explain more to you when we chat.

The form requires that you write your residential address. The address includes the house number, the street name, the city, the state and the post code, where necessary. How street names and other indices are determined or allocated, I will tell you in our talk.

The column that I would like you to pay special attention to on the form is your State of Origin. I want you to understand this very well as it points to your root.

I live in this city and this state because I was born here just as you were born here. The economic gateway and access this state provides must have attracted so many residents/settlers to it. People would naturally drift towards where they seemingly get better opportunities of livelihood.

But my state of origin is a neighboring state, just few miles away. We will drive down there someday and possibly enjoy some nights there so that you can get acclimatized to your root and see your people. Fortunately, MyPD comes from the same state as mine, although we met here in this state.

Within a state we have local governments; in some countries they are referred to as counties or municipals. There are cities, towns, in some cases, villages and settlements. You will understand better what they all look like when we go visiting my native city.

The people we have as neighbors are from different states as there are many states in this country.

The country is the overall umbrella for the many states in this country, just as there are many countries in the world. The world is the globe where all countries are located, states make up a country, local governments make up a state, cities make up a local government, and villages/towns make up a city. I hope that is not complicated?

You will wonder why the many divisions. They are important for easy administration and management.

There is also a fronted division as peoples' allegiances have been so fragmented which I don't want you to bother yourself about as I know you will come across so many bigots in your life as you grow.

Most importantly, always treat everybody with fairness, regardless of whatever cloak they have around themselves. You will get to see so many of those watery bridles people put on.

Your allegiance is to God the Almighty.

I know you will enjoy your schooling as you are already gravitating towards knowledge.

I love you my son.

'Debayo Coker

YOUR EDUCATOR

𝒟ear Son,

I looked back in the morning when I had to drop you off at school. I wondered how you would cope in that environment. It was your first day at school.

I started my primary education at age six. Before then, my mother had told me that when I was about three years old, I would cry whenever I saw my older siblings and neighbors going to school, wanting to go with them. So when I started at six, it was with so much fervor. Throughout my school days, I loved the experience.

I am delivering one of my many responsibilities to you as a father and I thank God for this great opportunity to be alive and endowed to carry this one out.

I chose this school for you after a thorough sleuthing of schools around here. It is a school that I know you would be proud to have on your Curriculum Vitae, not because of its aesthetics but because of the qualitative education it doles out and the crop of alumni it has produced are doing well in various fields of life.

You will meet a lot of people, especially students, from different backgrounds with different orientation and ways of life due to their upbringing. Son, you have no choice but to interact with them. Some of them will want to rub off on you and some will learn from you. Either way, you should always remember the son of whom you are. Always maintain the standard with which we have brought you up thus far. Do not be equally yoked with what is considered an aberration no matter what consideration you may want to give to it. Do not get me wrong, you will interact with them but let them learn from the virtues that are loaded on the inside of you. Let their parents come to school and say they will like to meet that boy that has so positively influenced their son. Remember my prayer for you that you will impact your generation positively?

Also, know that you will develop new friendships and amongst them you will have the best that you will refer to as BEST FRIEND. Usually, this person is a soul mate. I'll share my experience with you on this.

During my secondary school days, I had a very good friend. We are still friends till date though we have not seen face to face for a very long time now. The reason for that decision I will share with you later not through a note though. We were so close that if he was few miles away and he said something or thought about something I will feel it and decode his thoughts: telepathy.

When we left secondary school and I went to the university in Ile-Ife, which is several miles away from Lagos, he stayed back in Lagos to continue his life. Each time I would think in my heart that I will like to see him he would show up in Ife at most two days after my thought as he would tell me he felt like seeing me hence he came. Same thing with him. I would leave Ife to see him in Lagos each time he thought in his heart that he felt like seeing me: something will just unsettle me in school and I would feel he should be able to help. We were so connected.

Son, you will see how much you will get to love this friend of yours that you would treat him like a brother. Anyway, it is all a matter of time.

When you meet this friend I will like to know him. I will be so happy to have him around too as a son. After all, he is my son's friend. I will also like to meet his parents, know his house, understand his background, know the values he possesses and carries around. I will tell you why this is so important.

My friend and I used to be bullies. You ask who bullies are. Well, I do not need to scare you. They are those boys that will pride themselves as the powerful ones in school, tormenting other students. Sometimes, they employ vices to perpetrate their supremacy. Your father was like one of those bullies but I was not violent. Son, I must confess to you it is not a good way to live. It is never right to torment other people. Your code is far better than that Son. I will enlist you into a martial arts class not because I want you to start beating other children around but for your self-defense. You need it.

You will learn various subjects in your primary school. Take them serious as they are so fundamental to laying a solid foundation for your academic pursuit and growth. So important are your school work and assignments. Your teachers are always available to explain to you. Do not be afraid to let them know where you have knots, they'll help you untie them. Approach them with courtesy just as you have been taught and appreciate them adequately.

I have passed through that stage as well. What I did was that as soon as I got home after school hours, I would settle to work on my assignments even before I take off my school uniforms to shower and eat from Mami Agba's kitchen. Mami Agba was my paternal grandma; she was around to take care of me and my siblings till she passed in 1989. She would prepare my lunch and serve me steaming hot delicious meals. I will tell you more about her during our bedtime stories.

Those many books you see in the study are not just there for decoration, they are meant to be read just as I have read them all, including your mother's law books and journals. You too can start reading them one after the other as reading strengthens your academic and pleasure instincts. You will be able to understand the world around you as it is serendipitous in reach. Read my son.

MyPD and I are always approachably open to help you with whatever schoolwork that you may have us explain better to you.

May the wisdom of God continue to increase in you.

I love you son.

'Debayo Coker

CLEAR THE PASSAGEWAYS

𝒟ear Son,

How was your night? I had to leave the house very early today so I could not see you. Even MyPD got her parting peck still in bed.

I saw that you had fun last Saturday. Habitually, the last Saturday of the month in this state is taken as Environmental Sanitation day. That was what we fulfilled. Clean the whole environment. It is a noble monthly activity that has been with us for some time.

I liked the novelty we put into the last one.

We went down the road, just you and I, with our tools, to the canal, down the street, to remove those items clogging the easy flow of waste waters. You sprinted to work. Your very first community work.

I am sure you will do more of that even when there is no commendation from anyone just as the ones you got from Mr. Atkin and the other neighbors when they came to join us when they saw that we were working to ensure the flow of the drainage. That is how good neighborliness is built.

Son, I will permit you to go out this morning or in the afternoon (since today is your mid-term break) to see as the water now flows freely into the canal; be careful when you go so that you don't fall into the drainage. You will also notice that the stench in the neighborhood is no more. And if you will also observe in the next few days there will be less or no more mosquitoes as mosquitoes breed in stagnant water.

There is always a gurgling feeling that one gets from doing good. "It is good to be good", always.

Have a good time enjoying your mid-term break and be careful when you look at the water flow in the drainage.

Be the light or hold the torch that will illuminate the path for others.

I love you my son.

'Debayo Coker

WHAT IS THIS, SON?

𝒟ear Son,

How was your day and the journey back home? I am sorry I could not pick you at school today as I always do which was why I had to call the school management to allow the school bus take you home. It was because something came up at work and I was needed to attend to it immediately. Hope you had a smooth ride home with the school bus?

Now let us talk.

I came in now and found you sound asleep. Sorry I woke you up. You must have gone to bed when you saw that I was going to get home late. That was so thoughtful of you; early to bed early to rise.

I came straight into your room to see you and I unzipped your school backpack to hide some surprise items but I found something surprising to me in there.

You are awed? Don't worry we will talk about it.

That magazine is X-rated son. It is for people who are eighteen years old and above. You are just nine years old.

You explained that it was your friend that gave you to keep for him; That he said he took it from his father's shelf; That he wants you too to read it; That he is your good friend.

All well.

Those pictures are not for someone your age. You are too young to handle such views. I will be glad to meet your friend in your school tomorrow and I will be happier to finally meet the parents of your good friend so as to tell them to keep such materials far from the reach of young boys like you.

And son, for no reason at any time should you take anything from anybody to help him hide or keep. OK?

I have kept your surprise gift in your bag all the same.

You may go back to bed.

I love you son.

'Debayo Coker

WE HAVE A TASK

Dear Son,

I can see the shine of God all over you as you grow; happy is a father watching his son grow to becoming a man. God's grace continues to be upon you.

We have a task that we must do together.

You will be having a brother very soon. A brother is another male child from your parents. Yes, a brother.

We will have to set up the green room for him; the crib and the pen. I am sure we should be glad doing that together to welcome another child into the family. Super!

You are the first fruit of my loins. Your brother is a great addition and you will be so glad to have him around as a brother. His growing up will provide you the ample opportunity to understand how you have grown to the stage that you are now-A firsthand experience.

Let me tell you how brothers behave to one another and what they do for one another.

You see your uncles? Those are my own brothers. Uncle Similoluwa is my elder brother, and Uncle Lamide is my younger brother. I will tell you about my sisters subsequently.

I grew up bonding with my elder brother while my younger brother gravitates towards me. We went to the same primary school but Uncle Lamide and I had to change our school to another one when the family relocated. I will tell you the reason why we relocated subsequently. Everything I promised to tell you, I will tell you. Hold me to my words son.

We shared a lot of things and moments together. We were like three musketeers. As you can still tell each time they come around we share and play together even till now. You are wondering Uncle Simi with his grey hair could still play. Son, the blood that runs in us is the same. No matter how old he may seem to you he is my brother and I know where to kick start him if I want him in play mode. You see Uncle Lamide come into my house and say "Bayo I need your car" despite him having his own car; do not mind him; he is a spoilt boy…LOL.

One day on our way from school, Simi and I settled a bully that had been harassing Simi in his class. Do you know what we did to him? I better leave it to your imagination son. But I could tell you from the next day Simi enjoyed a breath of freedom from him. I have been so unlucky not to have a bully because I wonder what he/she will be treated like.

I tell you again, many years ago, a friend of Lamide's was trying to be rude to me, I watched Lamide stood up and protested that he would never accept such brisk rudeness from a friend to his brother. That is one of the things brothers do to one another. They protect one another from external aggression or oppression.

Let me tell you more.

While growing up, the trio of us played some games. Simi was at a polytechnic, I in Ife and Lamide back at home working immediately after his secondary certificate examinations. I took Simi's clothes, gave him mine and also do some sorting in Lamide's wardrobe. Son, we were like chameleons (not in character as our mother taught us better than that) at those times. Those made us appear rich with seemingly new clothes all the time.

Brothers share things in common. Even secrets are best kept as secrets amongst brothers.

Daddy Mi hates cockroaches so badly. He would run at the sight of its flight. We once pranked him as the three of us connived one day he wanted to flog Simi. We raised a false alarm as he raised his whip: we shouted cockroach, son, you needed to see that old man in flight. Brothers play together with their father.

Am sure you are going to do more than those three boys put together to make your brother comfortable.

I know you have a lot to share with him having read some notes before this. I hope you share them and our chats too with him.

What binds you is blood and blood is thicker than water.

I love you my son.

'Debayo Coker

AUNTY KORE

𝓐lexander Adesire Oluwalonimi Petrus Adebayo-Coker,

Omo Ade- a royal child. You are clad in glory. Princely are your ways. Kingly are your deeds.

I deviated from my usual opening this time to call your names in full because I want you to be enraptured.

I saw your reaction the other day when you were giving your clothes to Aunty Kore to wash for you, as well as when you raised your legs as she swept the floor under your feet the other day.

Again, you watched every day as Uncle Charles washed my car. I know you may seem too young to understand some things but the earlier you start grasping a hold on life, the better.

You know Aunty Kore comes in the morning and leaves in the evening. It is because she is married and has her own family, husband and children. Sometime I will invite her family over so that you will get to meet them.

Do you know why I am telling you this?

The same way your mother is Mrs. Adebayo-Coker is the same way Aunty Kore is Mrs. somebody to some man somewhere. The same way we gave birth to you is the same way Aunty Kore gave birth to her children. You now wonder why she has to be work with us as housekeeper.

I will tell you.

Let me start with Uncle Charles. He is a National Diploma holder. He used to work for an Insurance Brokerage firm. He lost his job along the line due to the economic crunch the firm suffered and he was left with no job for a very long time that it became so uneasy for him to survive. He got involved with some people and together, they adulterated and sold petroleum products. They lived large. One day he got home to find his house razed by inferno. His wife, daughter, his certificates and other belongings were all consumed in the inferno. He later gathered that it was the fuel that he stored in the house that caught fire and razed his life down. He lost his mind but thank goodness that he found Jesus along the line and gave his life to Christ. He is a clean man now. I can testify to that.

You see Auntie Kore. She used to be a full time housewife, that is, a woman that does no work but waits on her husband for every of her needs. Her husband used to work with the Railway Corporation. Due to mismanagement of the government parastatal, so many people were asked to go, that is, they were retrenched. Her husband inclusive. When the husband could not provide for the family as he used to do and could not secure another job due to his age, he bowed to frustration and took to the bottles, meaning he started to drink. His excessive consumption of alcohol led to health complications for him so he is lying critically ill in the hospital now as we speak. Aunty Kore had to beg for alms from people so she can take care of her sick husband and children. One day she met your mother who discussed her with me and we decided to employ her. You can see we have a washing machine for our laundry, a vacuum cleaner for the floor, a dishwasher for the plates, so it wasn't really necessary for us to employ her but to help take her off the street, we took her in.

Son, do you like the stories that you have heard?

You shook your head to indicate a NO.

Good.

I shared those experiences with you to let you know that in life there is what is called reversal of fortune. I am sure you remember my own story that brought about giving you that circumstantial name ADESIREMI. Go back to the first note I wrote to you if you have forgotten.

We are not the determinants of our destinies, we only trying our best to work it out. God knows best. Anything could happen to anyone any time. But we pray good things happen to us at the time.

I will also share my profound observation of a friend and his son. I am sure you will get to meet both of them in time. Kenneth and Makhena, father and son respectively.

Kenneth is a very wealthy man, a property mogul in the USA. Makhena is his only child. One day I asked him how Makhena is doing. He said he just went out to work. At that time he was barely your age. I probed further hoping that he was going to tell me he has made the young chap a manager or a director in one of his companies but he disappointed me. He said he has gone to work to earn his own money by mowing their neighbors' greenery.

Wow! I exclaimed. Kenneth made me understand that no doubt Makhena will end up inheriting all of his assets but if he doesn't know how to work to earn his own money, he would not appreciate what is committed into his care. Great idea!

Son, I want to borrow that idea from him. Don't worry I am not going to send you to mow to earn your money. No.

Henceforth, Son, you will be hand-washing your own clothes, vacuum the floor and mow this lawn of ours. That will be all for now.

I used to be a member of the Boys' Scout Movement. I am sure you have heard of that movement. Their motto is BE PREPARED. They engage in so many lofty activities to advance our world. They train boys to be prepared for hardships of life that may show up at any moment of life. I will encourage you to join them.

Also, you may have to learn to join the public transport once in a while back home from the school. You are wondering why I am exposing you to all of these, especially when abduction is as rampant in our society as it is? Well, son, no eyes of abductor, serial-killer, ritualist, and armed robber will see you because you bear the mark of Christ in your body. There is nothing to fear.

If not for anything, you need some street sense to survive in this harsh world. You need to know that there are some people that live far below what you take for granted. There are people that want what you have even if just for few moments. You need to interact with them. Approach them with respect and love my son.

Never depart from the training you have been given from home because that is your license to depict the side of the street you belong and will be asked of you by the people on the street if you tend to be like the people of the street.

Affection for them will help you understand their psyche. The man who remembers others, remembers also his creator. There is no lesser person even though social classes may be there. The same way they strive to have a good life is the same way we strive to have a better life.

Respect people regardless of their background and position. They are human beings like us.

I wish you strength in your sojourn.

I love you my son.

'Debayo Coker

WHAT! FUNDAMENTALS CONTINUE.

𝒟ear Son,

I am pleased with your academic advancement, the growth of boiling quest for knowledge, as well as your intense love for the things of God. I am fascinated.

The other day you came home with some group of boys that you introduced to me as your classmates. The only one I could recognize out of them all is your longtime friend. I am sure you thought I would still be in the office at that time. Well, I needed sometime alone that was why I had to come home earlier than usual that day.

Those boys looked good, clean and spoke good English just like you. Did you guys fish one another out to strike friendship? Well, it is expected as your school boasts of qualitative students.

But son, let me tell you pointblank, whenever you are bringing anybody to the house, teach them that whenever they see an elderly person in the house, they should prostrate and greet the person.

Let them know that Aunty Kore and Uncle Charles are part of the family and not just ordinary aides. Let them know we accord due courtesy here. I am sure you don't greet their parents standing when you go to their homes. You were not taught that way. If you greet them by prostrating and they ask you why you did what you have just done, tell them that is how you greet an elder in your culture.

Also, I heard them anglicize your name as they called you ALL DESIRE. Son! That is not the pronunciation of your name. Your name is ADESIREMI, to mean, arrival at my breakthrough. I have tried to add some aesthetic to it by prefixing it with AL, a clip part of Alexander so it looks AL-DESIREMI.

Son, the name people call you goes a long way in influencing your life. It is my responsibility as a father not to allow you to be called a bad name or given an alias that depicts brutality.

If you allow to be crudely tagged then you may be deviating from the path of excellence that you have been towing till now.

You may have observed that in all of my notes to you so far, I never and I will never refer to you as a kid just as I don't call you, your siblings and any other child a kid. Do you know why?

One of shared meaning of 'kid' includes a young goat. So why would I select a name that share its meaning with a young goat for my child. If I do that in the name of faddism, expectedly, such child would have shared characteristics of a goat. You are my son. Not my kid. How you are addressed influences how you behave.

You sneezed many times when you came in. That may have been a sign of health hazard. You may have caught cold because I saw you come home without buttoning up your shirt. You may have walked home in company of your friends, as I see that some of you were trying to show-off your broad chests to the world.

Son, you do not need to open up yourself to health hazard walking in the cold without being properly dressed. Apart from the health hazard you easily lose public respect because the way you are dressed determines the way you are addressed.

Dress neat always by wearing your clothes properly; use your accessories correctly: your belt on your waistline and not below, tuck in your shirts when you have to; a shoe to be worn as a shoe and not otherwise. You will look finer, sharper and respectable that way.

Son, you did something that I must also address here. It is so heart lifting to see a young man's quest for knowledge so intense. I will encourage and motivate you and your friends in every way I could to make sure you get sufficiently encouraged along such a noble path. "Supposedly", the quest for knowledge is never static.

Anyway, that is why I open my study to you and whoever wishes to use it. However I do not remember permitting you to give my books out to anyone, neither as an outright gift nor as in lend-lease, so why did you allow your friends go with my books? As at my last check, the books still carry my names on them. I understand your explanation that they want to use it for further studies. Good. But know that whenever anyone wants to borrow anything in this house that you have not bought with your money or has your name imprinted on it, you must as a matter of responsibility, let the borrower know that the item is not yours and that you need to get the permission of the direct owner before you can give it out. In the case of the book you gave out to your friends you should have come back to me since I was in the house with you and even if I was not in the house, you know that I am always a phone-call close to you.

I want to lay a rule here.

I will do a reconcilement of the books in the study with my log and determine those books you have given out. If by this weekend they are not back on the shelf I may have to use your pocket money to buy them back. God help you, they are the pricey ones. That is no pocket money till you cover the full cost.

Hey, lest I forget, learn to keep record of things, even the receipts of important purchases. That is so important.

Get yourself ready, we are going for a picnic this weekend. Guess where? Secret…winks>

I love you son.

'Debayo Coker

ODD VENUES

𝔇ear Son,

Because you have honored me by updating the study and have it cleaned out God will crown you with greater glory and honor. Humankind will not cease to honor you. You are a blessing.

Now, if anyone is borrowing our books, you wonder I say OUR BOOKS. Yes, they are our books as they carry our surname. We own everything together, others in the family inclusive.

Anyway, let us learn to keep a record of borrowers so that the books don't get missing. You know this is one of the legacies to be bequeathed on our generations to come. Thumbs up son.

Now, let us talk about what happened during our picnic.

I saw that strange look on your face when we went playing, dancing and eating at those places. You want to know why we stopped at those points?

Ok. No P, just as your generation will stylishly write No problem.

Those children you saw - younger, about your age, and older, they are some peoples' children. They did not fall from heaven. And God is not wicked to have created them and put them in that position.

There are many orphanages in towns, cities and metropolis around us that we often drive or pass by but never bother about the children in there. Some of those children were abandoned by their parents due to one reason or the other. Am sure you heard yesterday of a new born that had to be brought there because the teenage mother passed at her delivery and no family member has come forward to claim the child. So many things will come to mind as to the paternity of the child, son, do not bother much about that as God knows best and He knows it all. Such children need love and care. As far as I know they didn't choose to be in that position. Come off it, if we are presented with the opportunity of choosing our paternity, no poor man will ever have a child. I am sure you may have chosen not to come to me.

So why inflict pains on someone that has no say in whatever situation he/she has found himself/herself? They need our love, care and recognition. It could have been anybody.

Also, at the hospice we visited, those special children there are gifts from God to their parents, just as you are to me. They are just down with an ailment or the other. Some of the ailments are treatable and those that are not are usually manageable.

Some great people you see or read about are either from an orphanage or a motherless home, shown love to by some people either by way of outright adoption or affection and care. Show them love in a family environment and you will see them thrive. We will visit more often henceforth.

We will also visit psychiatric and correctional homes on more picnics to come. Those places are not odds at all.

I love you Son.

'Debayo Coker

YO MOMMA!

Dear Son,

How are you finding your first year in the secondary school?

I believe you are catching up on the more advanced educational techniques and ways of teaching. Here, some of the techniques you have learnt in the elementary school will be called to use. Your spelling skills as well as your English composition and comprehension will also be put to use most times here. Do you know why? It is because you are growing to being a man. It is expected of you to be composed and orderly. You will get to see as time goes by.

Did I tell you one of the reasons you are sent to school, especially to come to a class housed within a block amongst other blocks occupying a wide expanse of land? I will let you know. It is so you can interact with other people of different class, backgrounds, religions, etc. You remember I have highlighted this to you superficially in a note I sent to you when you started elementary school? Well, here you will consolidate on the bond that you have built so far from elementary school and take it further.

Networking starts here, so do lifetime friendships. You see that once in a while I tell you that I want to attend a reunion meeting and you see my classmates come to the house when I get to host them on such meetings? Well, that is a sample of it.

You asked me a question the other day as to why and how some people could be so bold to abuse their fellow students to the point of mentioning their parents. Well, that is not new. It stems from their home training. Not all of those children are as groomed as you are, so learn to know the company that you keep.

Hey, son, I almost forgot to congratulate your friend and his parents on his entrance into the same secondary school as yourself. I will do that straightaway once am done with this note.

I promised you in my first note to you that I will not throw a chair in this house nor any other house. Let me explain that statement to you and what warranted that.

For easy understanding, I will like you to watch a video with me. You can even view the video on YouTube on your own. It was a video of some supposedly grown up men in our Legislative chamber. They exchanged fisticuffs so raw, they graduated to throwing chairs at one another and eventually tore the clothes of one another to shreds. My son, those guys are some children's fathers. They were supposed to be honorable men but what they did was not at all honorable. Worst for their family members, amongst whom are their children, the video is uploaded online for the world to see and for generations to come for reference.

If the children of such men are yo-mommaed in reference to that act, it won't be a lie because whatever one does it is being recorded, somehow. Various videos of such acts and of some other people who have been so creative with the truth but were later found out during panels of enquiries into their acts or their stay in office, abound online. You will find them interesting.

Let me reiterate my promise to you. I will not for any reason bring disgrace and shame to you.

I love you my son.

'Debayo Coker

NOT YOUR FAULT

𝒟ear Son,

I am happy at the way you make me feel proud. I could not hide it from the public when you cleared five of the seven prizes on the Prize Giving Day of your school. I stood up and said THAT IS MY SON. I am sure you saw me and heard that shout. It is because you have made me proud of you.

And let me also include here that I am so thankful to you for your attempt to help repair my laptop. It is so much appreciated.

I tell you my experience.

You know your mother loves baking. Cake making is her passion and lawyering is her profession. Just as wordsmithing is my passion and doing business is my profession. I will let you know more about that in time.

One day I wanted to surprise your mother as she was to return from a conference that day after being away for two days. I got into her baking booklet, wrote out a fruit cake recipe (you know that is my favorite) Winks. Then I went into her storage and started mixing, chopping and all of that. While I was mixing I forgot that everything that goes into baking has its own measurement but my overzealousness got the better of me. Instead of using two eggs, I added five and because of my cultural mentality that everything that goes into the mouth must have salt to taste well I added a table spoonful of salt. Instead of just a little scraping of nutmeg I used a big nut. So also were some other blunders.

Son, the cake that was to be a surprise became a poison. The outlook was scarily horrible that no one dared put it in his/her mouth; we couldn't even serve it to Brownie, our dog. Your mother appreciated my effort that day all the same, though the cake did not turn out right.

I like that you have me in your thoughts to want to put your Introductory and Communication Technology acquisition to use. You are appreciated.

But aren't you like your woeful -baking Dad? LOL. Instead of fixing just the power port the whole laptop is torn to shreds....hahahahahah.

Anyways, we have decided, MyPD and I, to enlist you in a Training School where you can obtain comprehensive technical training in Desktop Engineering during your vacation. It is to enable you have hands -on experience in computer repairs and maintenance.

What do you think? I will keep this laptop as it is now and am sure when you are done with your training you will come back to repair and couple back this Steve Job's toy. You should not allow any situation to defeat you son. Go back, get prepared, get fired up and launch at it again.

Additionally, I taught you Yoruba my son. What happened that you could not win the prize in Yoruba? I must have been teaching you how to write too much of English that I didn't put you through Yoruba comprehension. Though you speak it so well but that is not enough, we need to go a step further by making you a good writer of the language. It is part of your root.

I want to believe you still have your Spanish, German, and French speech banks untainted. Anyway, I know you have a photographic memory and will not forget a word. I saw the way you engaged my Spaniard friend. He has invited us to Mallorca again. But we can't go now as you have to start your training in few days at AES's, am sure you will like the experience.

I love you so much my son.

'Debayo Coker

WHY I DON'T HAVE A BENTLEY.

Dear Son,

How are you doing today?

Let me start by thanking you for the Father's Day message you sent to me. It gladdened my heart to read it.

I want to share a story from my Pastor with you.

He told us while preaching how he felt intimidated by the look on his son's face on the street of London. The young lad saw a good-looking man, about his father's age come down from an exquisite car. As the boy moved his gaze from the car to the man, and back to his father, it was suggestive that the lad was wondering how come his father was unable to buy that kind of a machine for a ride.

The Pastor in his usual sagacious tune, said he called his son beside and made him know that he could buy a better car but he would prefer his son attend the best private school in town, his family had a house on the mainland and another on the Island, his family had the best of things in the world, and that it was obvious that the young man that came down from the car may not have such a dream.

That humbled his son and made him have greater confidence in his father: a lot of sacrifice on his part to make his family comfortable.

Adesire, fathers are great blessings. They sacrifice a lot to make their family comfortable.

I love you my son, my friend.

'Debayo Coker.

LET'S TALK: FAST LANE

Dear Son,

I have been observing how rapidly the metamorphosis of becoming a man is fast appearing on you. The other day I heard a husky voice in the house and I was awed it came from you. Very soon we will be sharing the shaving powder. You are almost beating my height. Your mother is already raising her head before she sees your face. God has been so good to us. His name forever be praised.

There is a subject that we must talk about. I have been doing an intellection of the topic for a while now as I see that you are fast growing even beyond our imagination. Now I think it is high time we get it done with.

You remember I told you I would have loved to help MyPD out to bear your pregnancy for at least a while so that she could rest but I was not programmed to do that? Well, that and more are what we must talk about now.

There are some changes that will be happening to you physically and emotionally.

Physiognomically, you are getting finer day by day. A lot of people will look at you and relish your handsomeness. Even males like you not to mention the females. You are a handsome man

I told you I used to be one of the boys that maintained my constant seat at the back of the class all through my secondary school days. Truthfully son that did not affect my academic performance but it hurtfully halted my smooth sail. I will tell you about that in time.

Well, back to the story, I used to get attention from so many females despite my rebel stance. They would send notes and those that could not write a note would systematically make their intentions known. My fellow boys could not talk to me directly as they feared me to be "notorious". But, son, there was no violence that I was involved in.

The only thing that attracted some boys to me was my brilliance and since I had some huge boys on my side that were ready to do my bid in exchange for some academic favors, some other students who could not understand the relationship , even teachers termed us to be the notorious guys. I suffered a bit because of that tag.

I had my first girlfriend in my second year in the secondary school and we lasted for about a session and when I wanted a 'change-of-guards", that is jump to another girl, son, those two girls fought one another dirty. On the school assembly in the morning (a usual activity for students to start their day during our schooling days), I am not sure you guys still do that, these girls engaged one another in vociferation then graduated to exchange of blows. Expectedly they were taken out by the teachers to the principal's office and I was brought in to explain the part I played in the whole saga as the girls mentioned my name in their plea and counter-plea. Son, what could I have said in that kind of situation? I was sent home that day to go and fetch one of my parents likewise the girls. When my mother came she was baffled that I have already started living on a fast lane.

Son, if you start engaging with girls now you are going to start on a fast lane and that is too dangerous for you. You remember on one of our visits to the motherless homes, there was a boy I played with, for so long, as I got so drawn to him, particularly, on that visit. Well, he is a result of two teenage lovers that were still in secondary school. Apparently they could not care for him so they gave him up for adoption. Son, would you have loved to start your life like those guys?

Now let me tell you the effect of being so badly tagged.

I had followers. It started as a parasitic relationship at first as I had to help some boys out during examination period. Naturally, they got drawn to me and we became a gang as I practically became the ring leader.

In between I was influenced to have a drag from a cigarette in my third year in the secondary school. I was able to take drags of some other substances as well, I will tell you about them during our chats. But I must let you know son, smoking is so injurious to your health and the health of others. It does not just cut your own life short but the lives of others as well. So it is a two-way killing substance. Suicide and murder should be two crimes smokers should be held for.

Another injury that I suffered for being so badly tagged was during a protest in my secondary school. It was in my fifth year. One of the school blocks was so dilapidated and the railings had fallen off. On a certain day, students were loitering about the building corridor and attempts were made by one of the teachers to get them back into the classrooms.

Son, the way we were communicated to or instructed to do any tasks was by proper thrashing. Not the democracy you guys enjoy now.

To continue, there was a stampede while scampering for safe haven to avoid being caught by the teacher. The railing gave way and two students fell from the topmost floor of the two story building. For a while there was calm. Reflexively, your father led a school wide protest. I didn't know where that courage came from. Police had to be dragged in to dispel the riotous students as some properties were damaged in the process. The school had to be closed down.

For two weeks the school was locked and when we were finally recalled to school, each student was made to come along with his/her parent who signed an undertaking on behalf of his/her ward(s) as well as make a payment for damages on their behalf.

Expectedly, my father had to come on behalf of Lamide and I. Undertakings and payments were accepted for him but mine was rejected. My father probed to know why. He was taken aback when the school principal, I didn't even know he knew my name, mentioned my name and narrated how I led the riot. My father pled with him and assured him that I will be of good behavior thenceforth. My son, my father corrected me when he came back home in the evening.

You know what I mean; serious unrefined thrashing.

What I did by leading that protest was not that improper but it was so adjudged because of the tag that I had on.

Let me bring it to a close with yet another story.

During the third term promotional examination period, I fell sick after taking some papers. I was placed on admission for the rest of the period of the examination. I could not take some papers like Mathematics, Government and Economics. Apparently, I knew the implication because those subjects are so germane to my being promoted to the next class. I pleaded with my mother to follow me to beg the school authority so that they allow me write the exams that I missed because it won't be fair that I will not be promoted not because I failed the exams but because I was not able to make it to exam venue due to my state of indisposition.

Sweet mother, she went with me. Luckily, the Vice Principal was a church member as they got to know during their conversation. The VP said her hands were tied as the Principal was not in town as he had the final say on such issue. You are wondering why we didn't call him on the phone? The luxury of mobile phone was not available then my son. Nigeria became connected to the GSM satellite in 1999. This happened in 1997. Well, the VP advised we could approach the teachers of the subjects and if they would be willing to conduct the exams for me at their own discretion, then the school will accept the result. My mother swung into action. We went to the government teacher and she expressly conducted the exams for me as she confessed that she knew I was going to pass the exams either then or now. The economics teacher also conducted the exam for me. I was left with almighty Mathematics teacher. I met a brick wall.

The math teacher was an old man from Ibadan. With his strong accent he would stroll into the classroom and teach us. I must confess he knew his onions. But with his accent I have pranked him so many times. I made him the center of humor each time he came around to teach us. He caught me doing that one day. He was not happy.

He vehemently refused to conduct the exam for me. Though he confessed that he knew I would pass, he said he needed to teach me a lesson.

Son, mathematics is a must-pass if one must be promoted to the next class during my time. I am sure it is still the same till date.

I could not be promoted to the next class alongside my boys. A peacock had lost its feathers.

Note it was not because I failed that I was not promoted, it was because of the tag that I bore.

Watch the company you keep my son. Learn from my mistake.

I love you son.

'Debayo Coker

ON YOUR OWN

𝒟ear Son,

How are you finding the whole process of maturation? Interesting?

I want you to have a feel of something that was why I had to stop you from going to school from home. Your letter from boarding school is so interesting to me when you tell me you are now realizing the reason I had to make you hand-wash your own clothes. You also mentioned you now use your martial arts skill so efficiently.

I was initially worried when you told me you are putting your martial arts skill to use as I thought maybe you have become a harasser of some sorts. But gladly I archived your note as I finished reading those lovely lines of yours just as I have kept others so safe, I believe you are keeping all of mine as well.

Well, my son, so is life. Some men are effeminate. They are sissy-like in their ways of life. You said the guy who is your senior in the school and the captain of your dorm had come one night to sleep close to you and that the next day he had called you into the hostel during prep when other students were studying. That he had touched you in a manner that you didn't like. I like those words that you used: HE TOUCHED ME IN A MANNER THAT I DO NOT LIKE.

Yes, people like that abound. Some of them will try anything to get to you. Gifts, affection, name it, all sorts, and sometimes they may even be violent with you just as you said that senior tried before you knocked his frontal tooth off. Son! Have your knuckles become that strong? Good one. That is one of the lessons I wanted you to learn when you were enrolled for that Martial Arts class; again it keeps your body fit and shapely. Go on boy; defend yourself against what you don't like. Stand up. Fight. For your rights if you have to.

I found your note more enthralling when you told me some seniors also tried asking you to empty your own provisions to fill their own lockers. You said you refused vehemently. They were amazed how you got the boldness to refuse their commando-style order. You said they let you go when you were about to raise an alarm to invite the dorm master. I like that so well. But next time son, be the voice for the voiceless you should have raised the alarm all the same.

Do you know why? All those other children that were so robbed of their provisions will fall back on you because they know you have and that will strain your little resources. That should be your watchword in life. Try to help others attain whatever freedom they so desire and need so that in turn you, yourself, will be free.

I have been invited to your school to see what you did to that senior whose tooth you knocked off as I was informed via a phone call by your principal that his parents are planning to press charges.

I am coming to your school this weekend to meet the parents of the boy. I will be there with MyPD.

Son; I will teach his parents how to train their child uprightly. I don't care his sexual orientation as long as he doesn't come near my son who does not agree to such a way of life. I will let them know that whatever he suffers from in his head should be curtailed within his head and not to be tried out with my son.

I may help them to pay for some artificial teeth if they may agree but if they insist on pressing charges I am sure MyPD will do anything to stand for her son. Her service comes priceless.

Son, I will make your principal and the parents of the boy know that if that "kid" of theirs is not properly warned and comes back to you to inflict any bodily harm on you, I will, personally, inscribe double of whatever mark he may leave on you on his parents: I will sue them for dereliction of duties or for shirking their parental responsibility, am sure MyPD will fix that up somehow.

You are my son and nobody dares threaten you. I rode them like horses.

A survivalist takes whatever comes to him/her and learns to live by it. Not a way of life to emulate Son. You are a knight and you are called out to rule. Be bold. Defend yourself as long as the cause is just. Keep defending yourself; you have the cover of the almighty God.

I will see you this weekend Son.

I love you.

'Debayo Coker

YOU ARE MY SON

𝒟ear Son,

It was so good to see you the other weekend that I came to iron out issues involving your senior, his parents and ourselves. It was a great opportunity to see you again. I miss you, especially our chats.

Your brother is fast growing as well as he will be sitting for his secondary school entrance exams in a fortnight. I am happy you guys are becoming men.

You apologized profusely for soiling my shirt the other day when we both could not resist the sight of one another and we magnetically hugged each other at your entrance.

I am sure you must have forgotten to wash your hands and have a change of clothes when the news came to you that I was waiting for you at the Principal's office.

I had wanted to come to meet you in the farm where I was told you were working but I had to change my mind as I don't want to burst into your privacy unannounced.

You came running straight to me and I could not resist ignoring your principal to stand up to hold my son again after a while. My shirt was smeared by the time we were done hugging for close to six minutes. Mehn!

Did you notice the look on the face of your senior's father? He was wondering why we were holding one another as if we have been apart for that long? I saw him when he came in and I saw his child come in afterwards. They greeted one another like some grudge existed between them. What?

You are my friend. My brother. My son.

I will hold you and show you off to the world. I am so proud to have you as a gift from God. That was why it didn't matter when you smeared my shirt. I could always wash it when I get home. The worst that would happen is to cancel whatever appointments I may have slated for that day after my departure from your school. But I can never wish you away my son. My blood runs in your vein.

The mother of the boy was so disappointed when you shared your story, how their son tried to harass you and take away your dignity. She felt so disgraced. Son that is what some children bring upon their parents. God bless you as you have never and will never disappoint us.

You could see they were the ones that even apologized to us at the end of it all. They have befriended us and we have invited them to our home. We will fine-tune the meeting day and I will let you know how it went when you come home.

Try as much as possible to call your senior whenever you want to pray. You do not need to talk about what happened between you two to anyone again. A friend's dirty linen should not be shown to the public. We have agreed with his parents to hold prayer sessions for him. In fact, that is what we will talk about when they visit.

Dear son, I am sure you know each time I make this announcement it comes with some steamy seriousness. Yes, this one is no exception.

Your principal told me in confidence what you did. She said you have not been found wanting in whatever way. She tried to justify your action but I must speak to you about it.

Well son, I understood when she reiterated your narration as to why you did what you did but I must let you know it was a wrong step taken to remedy a situation. She told me how you went in connivance with other students in your class to burst the lockers of those senior students that have been oppressing you in the dormitory.

Son, it is stealing. Yea, right, they have been stealing from you, taking your provisions and all other things but you all should have come together and reported the case to the authorities in charge of the hall.

She claimed you had to do that when you saw that fellow students were hungry and you had no provision to feed them. Son, I know the school provides three square meals for you guys. The provisions you guys bring from home are snacks and not the main meal so, when you say people complain of hunger, it is not a tenable reason to do what's wrong. Remember I told you to watch anything relating to food?

My son, if there is any reasonable issue, you need not hesitate to let me know. I will let you have it in reasonable time if am unable to provide it pronto.

Do not deviate from saving excess of whatever you may have, just as I taught you many years ago when I met you with about seven wraps of chocolate which you were about to consume at once because you were gifted them by an aunt of yours.

Learn to keep some on the side because a time will come when it will be useful.

I love you Son.

'Debayo Coker

WE HAVE A GIRL

𝒟ear son,

How is your study going on? I am sorry I could not drop you off at school as usual. I know you will understand. Duty calls. Mr. Fernandez sent your favorite chocolate and other goodies. I will have them kept safely for you until you come home during the mid-term break. Your brother and sister send their love. Wonder how you got a sister because MyPD was not pregnant when you left the house few weeks ago? Well, she is a blessing from God: a plus.

We all went on our routine visit to the orphanage. An infant, about few hours old, was brought in just at about the time we entered into the premises. She was looking tenderly fresh just as you appeared in your first pictures.

She is an innocent child brought into the world to have a life of her own through the rabid rape of a daughter by her own father. That is how bad it is Son. Some fathers are like that. They sexually molest their own sons and daughters. So unfathomable, but it happens. May God not allow our sense of humanness be depraved to a level of animalism. My Son, say AMEN. You are becoming a man.

Before then, as we see, MyPD and I have been considering that your brother too will soon go off to school like you. More so, MyPD has been protesting lately, being the only lady in the house, that she wants us to have another shot at making a baby which I have tactically rebuffed because I don't want her to go through child labor again; I fear that too many visits to the labor room is not good for a woman, and, even for the psyche of a sensible man. So we thought it best to adopt the girl and treat her as our own.

God answered us through her. You know whatever you ask from God with a genuine purpose and clear heart, He will provide an answer to.

Your brother and I have set up the baby room for her. All your toys and more that we bought for your brother have been washed and set in the pen for her. You see why I taught you safekeeping?

We did not spend so much money to buy things that she will need because we safely kept the ones we had before her arrival. We had to buy new clothes as you know the entire baby clothing we had were boy's. MyPD had even given them out in faith that if she ever got pregnant again, it will be a girl. I doff my hat for her faith.

I promised you I will tell you about my sisters but before that let me tell you some things about your grandmother, my mother. You have not heard this part of her story. This one is so different from when she had to sell all her things to make sure I started my university education.

Well, the very first and only time I was fearful, after I had been betrayed by people I trusted, in my life I ran home to the bosom of my mother, as I know whatever the case may be she will never give up on me, and trust me she comforted me and prayed like no other time. After it all, I regained confidence that has kept me thus far to face whatever the odds of life may be. That is the great strength in having a mother, a wife, a sister and a daughter.

My sweet sisters Adeola; Aderonke; and Olaide.

Sister Deola is the eldest and the family's first child. She is the mother figure for everyone now after the passing of our mother. While growing up, she bathed us all, she cooked our meals and fed us.

There is a story I would have loved to share with you presently about her but I am not sure she will like me to share this with you through a note. Don't worry; we will talk about it when you come. It is a story about how we wrestled our freedom from her, Simi and I especially. Uncle Simi could tell you the same story. Am sure he would laugh if you ask him, so also would Sister Deola.

Sister Ronke is the second child. She is kind-hearted to a fault. Trust your dad. I explored the kind heartedness so well. But I never exploited them. She can give you her eyes as you can tell she gives you gifts all the times she came to visit.

Olaide, is the baby of the house. She came after Olamide. I hope you now understand the sequence?

Well, Laide is so good; my dear sister. She saved me so many times during my many escapades. We all bond so well as a family. You can tell when they come around and when we go visit them.

One thing that I did for all of them was to police them all around. I remember being a chaperon to Sister Deola on many outings at the behest of Daddy mi. Initially, I didn't know that I was to explore that avenue to make cool bucks. I would get home and reel out to Daddy Mi how a boy stopped my sister on the way; whether she stopped or not, I would tell and possibly reiterate what they spoke about and that really piqued me against my sister. She would in turn beat me mercilessly at the slightest provocation. Son, she beat me "well well" as we say in Pidgin English to show superlative intensity.

Anyway, as I grew older, I got to understand what my father was setting me up to do. I was set up as a spy, a watchdog. I was bought over to the other side eventually and the perks of being a compromised spy on my sister were enormous: Cakes, drinks, and some coins exchanged hands. Sister Ronke was also in the bracket at that time.

For Laide, being the baby of the house, her own case was so special. We all watched over her. Even the girls like her. I remember almost beating up a boy classmate of hers that loitered around our house. After many queries and he could not provide suitable answers he almost got a spanking from your dear dad.

As we all advanced in age we got to know she is a lady and should be treated as one. Son, I became so close to Laide that Lamide and I got introduced to some of her friends. Don't ask me what kind of introduction…LOL

Well, I hope you were able to get the message out of the life experience I shared with you in the foregoing.

Men are so jealous in protecting their daughters and sisters. I have just one explanation for that as I know you may get to discover more reasons why that is.

Am sure you must have been engaging in some boy- talks already.

Some of the topics discussed are GIRLS GIRLS GIRLS.

Men tend to protect their own as not to be a focal point during boys' talk.

If you do not want your sister to be traduced in the midst of boys, you should refrain from badmouthing other peoples' sisters. If you want your sister to be well- treated, treat other peoples' daughters well. Show respect to a woman always. Never, for any reason should you raise your hand against a woman.

It baffles me how a man will harass/ assault his wife/girlfriend and such a man will go and fight his sister's husband /boyfriend who meets the same treatment he regularly doles out to his own wife/girlfriend to his sister. If it is so good to beat a woman, I will say a sane man will not deny his own sister a good treat.

I am sure you may have read or you will read some myopic articles about women. The common phenomenon to them all is that they tend to paint women as weaker vessels. Some will even say women represent the weakness of men. But that is not the truth. Gen 1:27 "So God created man in his own image, in the image of God created he him; male and female created he them."

God's plans are perfect.

No doubt they have different emotive and cognitive expressions, but where we think we are strong they are stronger. They handle things better than us depending on what you commit into their care.

We will chat more about them.

I hope you will protect your sister and share your notes with her just as you have shared them with your brother.

She will get special notes from me just as yourself and your brother.

I know you can't wait to meet her.

I love you my son.

'Debayo Coker

FISHING

𝒟ear Son,

How are you doing? It is fun.

I have a letter here from your Principal. She wanted my permission for you to work in the ICT Lab of your school as one of the student technicians, and it comes with pay. The marvelous thing is that you will be the pioneer lead of the novel idea by the school as you will train other children that are interested in acquiring the skill.

She informed me that you spurred the idea. She narrated how you volunteered to repair one of the computers in the Lab during one of the practical sessions. She told me you did an excellent job. Kudos, my son!

Now let us leverage on that.

I told you I will tell you about a gift and a profession.

I have a strong gift to string words together. I am in my happiest state when I do this. There is that indescribable satisfaction that I get each time I do that. Just as am concocting these lines to you, I so much love the feeling that comes with it. I can write poems, prose and drama. You will see that some books have my names imprinted on them in the study, the ones that I shelved under the label MY BOOKS. I so labeled that shelf because it houses books I wrote myself.

Your mom too derives so much pleasure when she bakes. You can see that despite her busy schedule she creates time to bake, even when the freezer is cake-loaded already.

I work in the creative industry as you can see.

Hey, let me chip in here. You will go with me to my office during your next holiday to repair some computers.

Your mother is a lawyer of about twenty years post- call. We will go with her to a law court one of these days. You know I told you that you need to see how lawyers talk in court?

What I do as a wordsmith and what your mother does as a baker are forms of gift: what we love doing whether we get paid for it or not. Come rain Come shine, we will continue to do it.

What I do as a businessman and what your mother does as a lawyer is called 'profession'.

Now let me try and draw a correlation.

You know at times people come to your mother to ask her to bake for them. And people do come to me too to help them write reports. More so, I get my books published for the public to read. That is to tell you that a gift could be monetized. Expectedly, if anyone sets up a business, it is because they want to make profits, that is, money.

You wonder why I can't just settle for wordsmithing since I can make money from the sales of my book and I derive so much joy doing that? Also, MyPD could settle to baking since people come to her to bake for them and she charges them.

Well, good observation son. But let me let you know that if you read the bible about the parable of talents told by Jesus Christ you will see that people are gifted in different and multiple ways and such gifting should not be allowed to go untapped.

Gifts are divinely imparted by God. The bible says, "He ascended up on high, He led captivity captive and gave gifts unto all men" (Eph 4:8).

Gifts can be sharpened by doing or interacting with people of like minds. I did not learn creative writing from nowhere, so also your mother did not learn baking from nowhere, so uncommon for a baker.

A Profession can be learnt by anybody who so desires. I learnt all about Customer Relations Management while working as a Telecommunication Executive in the Customer Service department of a telecom company. I worked in that company for seven years. You remember that I chatted with you about my story in that company. MyPD trained to become a lawyer. One could excel in whatever profession on chooses so long as one is driven by determination.

Son, let me quickly talk about passion.

Passion can be described as the intensity of belief one has in carrying out an action. Passion is always expressed through actions. For instance, a man that went to rob must have been so impassioned to do what he did. Likewise a woman that decides to start out in business must have been so fired up before she could take the step. That is to tell you that passion if not well managed, could be negatively expressed.

My son, passion is so much important in whatever thing you want to do. Fire yourself up to better your last result. Beat yourself to it. Know that you are not in competition with anyone but yourself. Conquer the fear that you cannot do it. Do not be a mediocre.

Congratulations on your first employment in life.

I love you son.

'Debayo Coker

CRACK KNUCKLE

𝒟ear Son,

Let me start this note with an idiom from our culture. You know idioms are metonyms that help in the push of mileage for words.

TI OMODE BA MO OWO WE O NI LATI BA AGBA JE'UN.

What that means is that a courteously well rounded greyhound will rub shoulders with the high and the mighty.

I saw you the other day when Uncle Akeem and Uncle Abbey came around to check on us and our new baby. You rushed and prostrated as you have been taught and have been doing from your tender age. I like that you still imbibe that. I saw you display it as well when you greeted your senior's parents. Hey, how is our senior doing? His parents never showed up. I guess they are too embarrassed to look into our eyes again. I can imagine the heaviness of the ignominy on them.

Uncle Akeem said you should stop prostrating all about each time you see him that you always make him feel too old as you are a full grown man yourself. He went further that you should henceforth call him AK.

Uncle Abbey kowtows the way of AK ....LOL. He chose AES as his new name. I hope you know AES means Abbey Electrical Services. You should know as the place you learnt your ICT maintenance and repair from is close to his office. You should have asked him on one of those occasions that you stopped by at his office to collect money for lozenges....I caught you there....LOL.

Don't mind those two. They are old men that refuse leaving the stage for you and me. Am sure you know I am not an old man. I am still young and even younger than those two that asked that you call them coded names.

Ak has grey hair already. He uses hair dye to keep it black. And if you will look AES closely you will see that he doesn't walk so fast. Challenge him to a race and you will find him out.

I can still jump, run, and bend down to touch my toes with no aid only that I cannot run for too long. But son that does not make me old like those guys. I am not an old man.

Ak and AES send their warmest love as they are here as I write this note. I let them read how I have betrayed their secrets to remain youthful. Their jeans-secret I call it.

I need to take my For Fortyplus medications now. MyPD shares the same medications.

We are not old.

I love you dear son.

'Debayo Coker

OF HAPPINESS. OF RICHES. OF WEALTH.

𝒟ear Son,

How was your journey back home? I have to send you this note as we were only able to Skype last night because we are separated by the boundaries and of the boundless time and space. I will be back home in a few days.

I overheard in the background after you left and MyPD came online to chat with me. I heard as you shared your experience with your brother and some friends of yours, as I would want to believe that is what they are.

Well son, it is important we talk about life fundamentals.

Happiness comes from being fulfilled doing what one is called out to do. Everyone with his/her own talent(s) and using same to impact their society positively. Anybody could be happy depending on the motivation.

Let me share an experience with you.

In the course of writing these notes, I had to run an errand for MyPD as she needed my help in some ways because of the weariness her state of pregnancy has confined her to which did not allow her and any other pregnant woman to be as active as they were before their being pregnant.

Son, I ran the errand so joyfully and I knew I oozed out wealth of happiness bringing smiles to the faces of the driver of the tricycle that conveyed me to the ATM point, and to every seller I came in contact with that day.

Do you know what is responsible?

It was because I was so happy that I was writing a book and not just an ordinary book. It is this noteography.

That is the nature and motivation of and to happiness.

Happiness is universal just as smiles, tears, sorrow, and death.

Riches are like having excess of quantifiable token(s). Lately, we could say excess of commodities like money.

Wealth could be taken to mean having so much abundance that radiates and transfers to people around you. Wealth swallows riches as the latter resides in the former.

There is nothing stopping one person from having these three.

A lot of people are poor and a lot of rich people are not happy because they fail to harness our God given talents to the benefits of themselves and humankind in general. That is why we have few wealthy men around in the world today.

Son, what you see on display in those Hollywood movies and musical videos are usually ephemeral riches. They are not real. They are the kind of riches that will develop wings and fly away as described in the book of Proverbs.

Wealth does not make noise. It shows. You see it oozing out to the fore from an inner satisfaction as displayed on the faces of the carriers of such abundance. It transcends to others in form of service to humanity. It is not necessarily materialistic.

There are many wealthy people in history that I can point you to but I will mention just two amongst them: Mother Theresa, MLK and Nelson Mandela. Study their lives and you will understand what I mean.

I love you son.

'Debayo Coker

BEYOND TIME

𝒟ear son,

How are you? You are now preparing to sit for your entrance examination into the university. How time flies…

You know I told you in the last note how boundless time is. Yes, boundless to the point that, men invented the watch to monitor time and funnily the watch that men invented now guides the lives of men.

But you know one thing? A man can live beyond time. Let me try to explain what I mean.

A dead lithium battery for example, you can still hold it in your hands but functionally it is useless. It amounts to nothing. That means it is dead.

Accept my use of Nelson Mandela again as an example. I believe you must have studied him by now. You saw his statue adorning different buildings when we went to the Rainbow Country, South Africa the other time.

Mr. Mandela passed on in December 2013, just a few months before your birth. Great man he was; a paradigm of modern day struggle who had a determination for freedom; an embodiment of selflessness. He has become a brand to the point that his customized shirt is being worn all over the world, even till date.

You could see that he has lost all physical attributes necessary to sustain life but he still lives on.

Through legacies, way of life, books, above all the great sacrifice that he made to make sure that the Rainbow Country attained self-rule. Read about him as his autobiography is in the study, LONG WALK TO FREEDOM.

I am sure Mr. Mandela is being read in some places by some people even to the darkest part of the world as I write this note and as you will be reading it.

That is the way we should pattern our lives by engraving our names in the sands of time through offering selfless service to humanity. Make history and not just "follow follow" as we say in our local parlance to mean another lazy conformist.

Is there anything you want me to assist you with to aid your study for the entrance exams?

I love you my son.

'Debayo Coker

GET FIRED

𝒟ear Son,

I wrote this note as a matter of urgency in response to the note you sent to me where you informed of your confusion and fear in preparing for your university exams as you feared the examiners may go beyond what you have known or have been taught in school as they are international examiners.

Son, let me make one thing clear before we proceed. I understand you can be confused at times but never for a second entertain fear in your heart.

Fear is a killer of so many good ideas and people. It may even cut the life of someone short.

"Cowards die many times before their deaths; the valiant taste death but once."- Williams Shakespeare

Have a Joshua-like courage, son!

You are confused because the examiners are external people coming from the British Council of Education. Is it because of where they are coming from or the color of their skin? If you have my earlier notes with you, refer to it and if not I want you to cast your mind back to a particular note titled, LET'S FILL THIS FORM. I made you understand the monadology of the world.

Son, where the examiner is coming from or what they look like does not matter as to bring confusion into you. The important task should be your focus-THE EXAM.

Dreams are your visions of what you want to be in life. If you must also know nothing good comes easy. You cannot fold your arms and expect things to fall into place. You must get to work to get things achieved. Be positive even in the face of adversity.

Let me talk to you figuratively.

Do you know you can jump from a high rise building without even recording a bruise? It is possible if you set your mind to it.

Do you know you can be a food supplier and yet be hungry? It is possible if your mind is not set to understand your abundance.

Let me share some experiences. They are not mine though as I read about them myself, somewhere.

As part of the Indian culture, once a boy is given birth to he will be gifted a baby elephant and a tree will be planted in his name, to mean he owns the elephant and the tree.

As the baby grows, the elephant grows and so does the tree.

The boy will be taught how to give out orders to the elephant and the elephant will be taught to obey his orders being the master of the elephant as the elephant will be tied to the tree, the stake.

Son, do you know the elephant at birth is at least six feet tall. And it grows to become a gargantuan creature?

But whenever the boy, regardless of how small he may be, commands the elephant to kneel down so that he can mount him, the elephant gullibly obeys and when the boy tours the town and returns home, he ties the elephant to the tree, its stake.

That is how the elephant, the boy and the tree live.

I am sure you notice that the elephant is the only creature so disadvantaged amongst the trio because he is the only one that is not living and realizing his potentials.

Whereas, as big as the elephant is, with just a shaking from him, am sure, the boy will fall off him and the tree will be uprooted. That is how much energy is inherent in the elephant, but he has been reduced to a life of curtailment.

Let me share another experience. Though I know what I, ordinarily, should do at this time is to encourage you to study hard, let us take some time out to understand what we have at hand.

A certain young man built a very beautiful aquarium loaded with a lot of different kinds of fishes. Then he introduced a kind of fish, (I can't remember the name as I write this note, I will let you know when I remember), the fish ate all other fishes in the aquarium. The young man was baffled and bought another set and immediately poured those into the aquarium the fish-eating fish ate them all. Then he came up with an idea.

He divided the inside of the aquarium with a glass. You know a glass is crystal and the brain of a fish may not even decipher a glass especially when she is inside water.

Well, our friend put the monster fish on her own on a side of the aquarium parted away from the other fishes on another part of the fish tank. As the monster fish launched herself to go eat another set of meal, she met a brick in between as her head was hit on the glass. She swam back and launched herself with gusto to grasp the meal, she hit a wall again and this time it hurt so badly she gave up. Thereafter, she gave up as the breeder left the partition for two weeks after which he removed the divide, by which time the fishes swim even closer to the monster fish with no attempt from her to harm them let alone eating them.

Do you know why she did not launch at them again? It is because she felt she will meet a brick wall and possibly hurt herself in the process.

That is what life is like sometimes my son.

We give up on our oars when we experience some form of adversity, just like our fish model. Some people may not even try to get things achieved at all for the fear of the unknown as typified by the elephant in the illustration.

There is abundance of strength on the inside of you, son, tap into it.

Pray as you prepare for the exams and God will direct your paths.

Death is inevitable but living is a choice. Many are alive yet they are not living.

I wish you success in all of your exams.

I love you son.

'Debayo Coker

WHILE 'U WAIT

𝔚elcome back home Son.

You have gone through and finished the rudiments of secondary school education. We can now call you a secondary school certificate holder but it doesn't end there as there is a higher ground to aim for..

While you wait for the results of your exams to come, let us work out something to get you busy. You need to channel the exuberance associated with someone of your age positively so that you will be better equipped for the next level of education.

I know what it means to be expectant. Waiting requires patience. And patience is not what you pray for, it is what you as a person must exercise, you can only ask God for His grace.

There is no way you won't have to wait for something in life. Nothing good comes easy. You will wait for investments to mature. You will wait for your crops to germinate. You will wait for pregnancy to become a baby. You wait for a child to grow to become a man or a woman as the case may be.

It is what you do in the gamut of waiting that matters.

One thing that is common to humans is that we doubt the abundance of the energy we have loaded within us. We believe we should just watch as things unfold; following the wind of life as it blows us. If we do that we will be like them that know not where they are going. The quantum of strength you have should not be compromised at all at any time.

Have plans while you wait.

My son, I want us to act as two matured adults that we are though you are two years away to be answerable. I will deal with you as one already. Do not hesitate to let me know your stand on what I am about to tell you.

I saw that you fixed my car the other day as you undertook the servicing to the minutest details. Son, I don't even know how to change my plugs. I will be downstairs by 7am tomorrow, God willing, and wait for you till 7:10am so that I can drop you off at an auto-center close by to my office in order for you to catch more experience, learning from the masters.

But if you don't like the idea, don't show up at 7:10am I will understand and that will not change anything.

Your choice.

I love you son.

'Debayo Coker

I SAW HER

Congratulations son!

Wow!

All glory to the almighty God to whom all praises must go. He heard my prayers and He answers them all.

In CREDENDUM TO MY SON, I prayed that whatever my achievements are, you will dwarf them in your adolescence by the grace of God. Son, those words have come to pass in your life, even in my lifetime.

I was so happy the other day when you not only came earlier than 7:10am, you were the one that waited for me downstairs. You sure will excel in all of your undertakings.

Your results came, both the local and the international exams that you sat for. Son, you beat me to it. The results are better than what I contemplated. I didn't write international qualification exams though, as I was almost reduced to a "local champion" due to the limits of the exposure of my parents. But God has been so good to me that He opened my eyes to see beyond my father's house and homeland.

Now you are going international with high flying wings as you did excellently well as evidenced by your results, all subjects with the topmost grades in each one of them. Now, you have scholarships from different ivory towers, internationally, to study any course of your choice. Great!

It is worth celebrating.

God will continue to show you His kindness.

Now let me ask you.

Who was that girl you dispatched hurriedly the other day as I drove into the neighborhood?

Common son, I saw her.

I will like to meet her. Talk with her. Invite her over this weekend.

I know she is your very good friend that you could not wait to break the news of your international scholarships to.

I know you have been calling and sending text messages to her of recent or how else can you explain using up those numerous phone cards I saw in the trash can in your room.

Son, a man was once a boy.

I love you son.

'Debayo Coker

NEV'LAND

𝒟ear Son,

How was your flight my dear son? It was your first time flying unaccompanied by MyPD nor myself. It must be a new experience for you, especially now that you will be staying overseas longer than the usual short visits that we have had in the past on our different vacations abroad, most of which didn't last for over 14days on each visit.

My friends, Kate and Jeff are Americans living in New Hampshire and Washington respectively. I got my firsthand experience of snowing from Kate as she put me through what it is like even before I saw snowflakes in their primary domain.

She told me to get some ice cubes into my blender, grind them, then I should dip myself into imagining a huge load of that everywhere on the street, so high to the point of covering up a car and such condition lasting a long period of time; better still, sitting up in my chest freezer for a long period of time.

I am sure you are experiencing some cultures that are totally different from what you have been used to before now. You will experience what is called culture-shock but not to worry you will get used to it with time.

You will yearn for MyPD's apron so much that you will feel like jumping on the plane to savor the flavor of her culinary acumen. It is called homesickness. Son, with time you will overcome that too.

I told you I was a bit spoilt by my mother. All of my stay in Ife when she was still alive, I would run home each weekend to be with her, am talking about traveling several miles forth and back. The only weekends that I did not travel to my mother were those that I had to write a class test or exams. It was not easy for me to be separated from my mother but here I am today, motherless.

Acclimatize yourself to the environment. What you enjoy today as a norm started as a new. Get used to the new you have before you, so that when your brother will someday come overseas to study just like yourself, you will help him settle in fast and also make him comfortable.

How are you finding the Ivory Towers there? Not like the ones we have here. I am sure you will dazzle them with your rounded ingenuity.

Hope you are in contact with your special friend?

Wherever you go God is with you. He is your father.

I love you son.

'Debayo Coker

PECULIAR

Dear Son,

I hope you are not getting distracted by anything there? Remain focused and the world will be at your beck and call.

I read your note to me about what happened. It is an experience of life.

You said you wouldn't have mentioned it to me if I hadn't asked in my last note since you have put it behind you already. So is the spirit my son. Shake off the beast!

Matters of the heart should be taken serious as not to get the heart artfully damaged. No pun intended.

Anyway, it shows how ephemeral and shallow people are in their pursuit of materialism and quick satisfaction.

That you did not buy a gift for someone does not in any way reduce the love you have for such one. An internationally-acclaimed day of celebration of love depicts some kind of insufficiency.

Love, as simple as the word may seem, does not need any coordinating or subordinating adjective to maintain or retain its meaning. It is simply LOVE. Just as a Christian does not necessarily need any adjectival qualification to be balanced, it is either you are a follower of Jesus Christ in deeds or not, no midway about it.

The new terms being employed by different kinds of people and organizations were symbolical parts of the veil that Jesus Christ Himself shredded when He cried with a loud voice before yielding up the ghost on the cross. Study more and closely about the life, the death, and the resurrection of Jesus Christ.

Well, we are talking of matters of the heart here.

That you give a flower, chocolate, or such other items do not indicate or substantiate love. Though there is no way you can love that you don't give just as it was exemplified by God through giving us His beloved son to die for us in order to reconnect us back to Him, but not all giving is backed by love.

Love is an everyday thing and should be celebrated every time not once-a-year faddist expression.

My son I love you just as the rest of the family loves you. So if anyone will walk out on you just because you couldn't afford to buy them a teddy bear on a particular day of the year, then help them hold the door open and don't forget to shut it once they've left. Good riddance.

You said you met another girl over there and she was all over you and affectionately available to you.

Son, when I saw those words you used, "my liver cut". You remember that local parlance of ours that means I was afraid?

You did the right thing by cutting off from her as you said she wanted you to go to bed with her.

Sex is a proprietary right within the confines of marriage and if practiced outside of marriage, it is fornication or adultery. I am glad you didn't fall for her.

There are two more things I want to point your attention to here.

You will meet some boys that will ask you to the clubs, nothing wrong in clubbing, as long as it is a good club as you see me go to clubs too. But when it is a place where you may be tempted to engage in some vices, I will urge you to RUN. Remember the story of Joseph.

Also, they will tell you to hitch a ride with them but stylishly ask to see their driver's license. This is important because you may be implicated if they were found out to be unlicensed due to their age or misdemeanor. You, yourself need to wait till your next birthday before you could be licensed to drive.

Guard your heart!

I love you son.

'Debayo Coker

POLITICS

𝒟ear Son,

With these notes I feel so close to you. Even when I receive yours through emails, I get them printed and filed so that I have them close to my side. I hope that is the same way you treat mine? Don't keep mine to your side alone commit them to your heart.

You said there are many things you see that you don't like. What have you done about them if I may ask?

In my observation, there is usually a power play in the world at all times, even far beyond what the ordinary lenses could see.

There are instruments of oppression which could be in the form of the military strength of a nation, economic power of a country in terms of her GDP and some other development indices: so many are the instruments.

Also, there are instruments of negotiation to gain freedom from oppression. Our irreducible resolve usually gingers us to determine what means to use to seek our freedom. But you must know that freedom can't be given if not demanded. Take for instance, the many declarations of self-rule that you have read about.

Freedom from spiritual oppression is primarily from knowing God through thorough study of His word and prayers. Kneel down and pray to Him and He will bring succor to your heart. I have to let you know this because there are so many complications being made more complex by seeking spiritual help from where there is none. Only God delivers. Don't be a feast for some people, who call themselves MoG or WoG, as I have not in my lifetime seen a man or woman that is not of God.

To seek financial freedom you must be wise enough to know what your environment needs/ wants and how you can capitalize on that to make legitimate cash.

As for political freedom, my Son, you must be involved in the struggle in order to get yourself liberated. Some people may use Machiavellian tactics but whatever you may want to adapt from Nicholo's THE PRINCE, don't be violent.

Let me share a chat that I had with a friend.

This friend and I engaged in some cerebral discussion and he got stuck and leaned towards the bible in order to get back at me.

He came from the viewpoint of providence in leadership as he said God plays a lot of role in the selection of leadership, which I totally agree to. He was happy thinking he had made a towering point.

I helped him with the book of Daniel 5; 21c "...God rules in the kingdom of men, and He appointeth over it whomever He will."

Trust your dad, I launched back.

Providence is not enough to sustain leadership and success in general; even in some cases providence only provides accidental leadership. One needs calculated tactics to maintain such breakthrough.

I made him realize there was a King called Pharaoh whom God destroyed along with whomsoever rode with him that day he pursued the Israelites that God had set free. I also pointed him to Kings Saul and Nebuchadnezzar, just those two amongst many, whose kingdoms were taken away from them just because of God's chosen people. My son, you are one of such chosen.

Do what you must legitimately do, to let your voice be heard as you have enormous potentials that can't be taken away from you. Don't just fold your arms and be committed to a life of servitude or allow other people's stereotypes determine your own way of life, decide for yourself the path you must go.

Be involved and be the change that you want.

I love you son.

'Debayo Coker

SEAFARER: NAVAL OFFICER

Dear Son,

You look cute in those pictures. You are such a bloke already. MyPD has reframed all pictures in the house to the currency. You need to see them.

You told me you were disappointed in your friend as he is dating your ex now. That you suspected they may have been seeing one another while she was with you. Well you may be right. And you may be wrong as there is no evidence to substantiate this claim or refute it as the case may be.

I have known MyPD for almost 20yrs now so if I talk like a lawyer it is because I am the husband of one. She can talk to you about CRM so well as well.

If you say she is an ex, I believe you should let her remain an ex, by letting her remain where she belongs-THE PAST. Don't allow what has gone by to affect your present. It has passed. Focus on the present. Take hold of the moment. Launch yourself as you project into the future. Whoever she is seeing now should not be your concern. Remain friends with her if it is workable between you two, if not wish one another best of luck in your future exploits.

I will tell you, some of the things that friends are for and what they will not do.

Friends watch one another's back. Maybe that is what your friend is doing for you if it could be established that he is seeing her.

A friend makes another comfortable in each other's company. If you are not comfortable with a friend, leave the scene. You don't call someone a friend and be suspicious of such. Anyone you are suspicious of can't be said to be a friend.

I will refer you to my short story, TRIUMPHANT ISLAND. I have it on the shelf.

A leopard can't lose its spots just as a chameleon also can't lose its inconsistency.

If it is not the original it can't be the original.

True friends abound.

I love you son.

'Debayo Coker

THAT IS MY SON

𝒟ear son,

I have never been prouder in my life than during your graduation ceremony. MyPD and I couldn't be contained as I jumped to shout it to the world.

You looked like an academician in your robe so I wasn't surprised when finally it was announced that you have been offered a Fellowship Award of the highest professional body in your field. Our joy was boundless when you presented the Valedictory speech being the valedictorian.

Do you know I struck a deal in the graduation hall?

I was approached by an old man who offered me his call card. I couldn't read it immediately, as courtesy would demand, as the joyful atmosphere in the hall, coupled with the butterflies that were flying in my tummy made nothing more significant to me, but when I finally read the card I found he is a top executive in the Silicon Valley. I will let you know what he talked to me about subsequently.

Your siblings made new friends.

MyPD too made new contacts.

You made us all proud.

I love you my son.

'Debayo Coker

STEER THE WHEEL

𝒟ear son,

How are you finding your job in the ivory towers? We had a smooth flight back home. Don't hesitate to send those two back home if they are becoming too troublesome for you. Anyway, they must get back home in two weeks from now so they can prepare for their resumption. Let them enjoy the company of their brother and hang out with their new contacts. They are under your watch.

Let me quickly tell you what the man from the Silicon Valley that I met on your graduation discussed with me.

He said he was there to draft the best your school produced to work with him. He made me understand he does that annually as he himself is an alumnus of that institution of yours. He also said he knew there were a lot of companies with plans to hire you especially when he heard that you have been offered a Fellowship Award. He sensed the competition to get you would be stiffer than what he envisaged hence, he tried to get to you through me. Wise man he was.

I assured him I will talk to you but the decision is yours to make.

You have always been the captain of your ship, I am only a guardian and we both must see God as our compass and anchor.

Son, you sure have many offers laid before you, just as many companies back at home want you to work for them so that you can help contribute your quota to the building of your fatherland.

Whichever path you want to go, I got your back.

I love you Son.

'Debayo Coker

HONESTLY, I DON'T KNOW.

𝒟ear Son,

How are you handling this period of your life? I must let you know that I have been through that way myself. She is from your rib.

You ask: if I said I have been there, then I should be able to tell you how I got through it. Well, honestly son, everyman for himself and God for us all. Discover her more.

MyPD is the most perfect wife I could have in this world. She has brought me so much joy and made me the best man in the world.

But do you know that there have been many times that I have wanted to walk out? Walk away to a place where I won't get to see her again? But I could not because there could never be a person, even if I traveled round the globe that could be so perfect for me as my wife, MyPD.

Before I met her, I lived the life of a bird: I went out whenever if I felt like it, no prior arrangement necessary, slept out without blinking. I clubbed and did all sorts of things. Along the line, I got married to the most wonderful person in the world. Definitely, I had to adjust to the new life of marriage.

MyPD came with her own codes. Her worldviews and mine were not totally aligned. It was a new position that I had to learn to adjust to.

Do you know you came the second year of our marriage?

My son, do a bit of mathematics. Add your present age plus two. Easy math. That is the sum total of our wedding anniversary. Over 20yrs.

Still I am discovering new things.

Learn to understand your wife.

Mind you, it is forever together at all times that you both swore to. Then, if it is forever, you must know that even 50 years in, the marriage is too short a time for you to start complaining.

We are all learners in this institution of marriage.

I will share a very wonderful tool that is pivotal in making you enjoy your journey through this path with your wife.

Learn to talk only inside your bedroom, whether you have a guest in the living room or not. Do not take your talk in front of any guest, not to mention taking it outside your home. Please, no third party involvement.

Remember, I asked the band to play "JUST THE TWO OF US" for you on your wedding day? That was symbolic.

I know you are a wise man who will not look at the cosmetics of a lady to choose from as a wife. Rather, you will consider her innate make-up which is more expansive than any superficial enhancements of whatever degree put together. Delve more into that interior make-up of hers.

I love you son and wish you success in your marriage.

'Debayo Coker

DISCUSSION CONTINUES...

𝒟ear Son,

How are you and your family? I hope you will bring my granddaughter to visit me soon. I do understand the tight schedule that you run as you work in the ivory tower, as well as being a consultant to different companies in and outside of the Silicon Valley. Recently you have been conferred with a professorial status in another university. But do not deprive me of seeing my grand babe again and again.

I recall how completely traditionally dressed I was when we took you before the Lord for dedication few weeks after your christening. I praised and danced to the Lord for establishing my household. I will continue to pray for you as you too should not relent in communing with God.

In furtherance of our family tradition which is to read the bible to our children from their tender age, please find enclosed herewith the Children's Bible that we bought for our granddaughter. Try as much as possible to read it to her hearing as it has been simplified and adapted to bed time stories. Catch them young.

MyPD will like to share her culinary skills with her daughter in-law so that in turn you don't have to feel homesick whenever you miss her meals. I cannot continue to lend you my wife for cooking purposes, instead equip your own. I have shared mine enough with you.

We will be meeting your sister's special friend this weekend. It will be a special moment in our lives as individuals and in the life of the family altogether.

We have a lot to talk about that will never be exhausted on the pages of papers that have ever been made and that will ever be made in human history. In the meantime, I want to seek your permission to do a compendium of your responses to the notes I have written to you so far. It is a two-way communication line.

You wonder why I have to seek your permission.

Well, I don't want to take advantage of our relationship to infringe on your proprietary rights. More so, it is your privacy and I must respect your decision if you do not want me to put it in the public domain.

Let's keep the line open to talk more often and I pray if the Lord tarries in His coming, we will be able to cover a lot of things as they are obviously inexhaustible.

Extend my warmest howdy to the rest of the family.

I love you my dear son.

'Debayo Coker

WHY I DID IT: THE EPILOGUE

𝒟ear Son,

How is the weather there, my daughter in-law and granddaughter?

I am glad you are in constant touch with MyPD and your sister to tap into their wealth of experience in handling that little girl of yours. Before you know it she will introduce you to her man. That is how fast women grow. They grow faster than us men. Anyway, God will guide her steps as I trust you won't lead her astray. Grandfather is always here to talk to her at any time.

You said some of your friends read some of my books, that there is even a particular one that follows my writings so passionately. That is lovely. You said he probed into why I have to publish our notes that were supposed to be kept between us.

He has a point but let me clear this once and for all.

My debut publication, SOCIETAL FRAGMENTS was first published in January of 2014. It is a book that addresses societal issues with focus on the girl child, education, cultural norms, politics, and workers' plights, to mention a few.

You should be able to talk more about it as I know you have read it. Some critics will point to some errors in the book. I have to point them to the title of the book, it has ERRORS in it.

This noteography is my second book. But if you can recall the opening part of this book: HE KNEW YOU: THE PROLOGUE, I talked about holding it in trust for you. Royalties from the sales of this book went into your education and now that you are a man of your own you own the book in its entirety. I will pass the account details to you via my Will.

I started writing this note about the same day a high priced literary competition announced its opening. I had a foreknowledge of the competition and had started preparing by working on a story of a brother who was separated from his family due to the Nazi policies in the old German nation but got reconnected to them through her boxing-loving sister as the man eventually became a boxer and had to cross the Berlin wall to fight in the region where his family resided. I titled it BERLIN SEPARATION. The script is still in my drawer in the study. I could not finish the script on time because I got stuck.

When this noteography came to mind, I contemplated expunging your name from it as it was part of the rules that the author's name must not appear anywhere on the submission as not to influence the judges decisions. Son, there is no way I will write your name on that script that my name will not appear as you see in NOW THAT YOU HAVE A NAME.

I could have found some fictitious names as substitutes of your name and the names of the different characters that I used here as they are all real, entered the competition, possibly won the prize which I needed so badly at that time, and lived my life; but son I banished that thought forever from my heart because you are so priceless. No amount of money can buy you for me.

All the characters that appeared in this book are real, though I put some of them into some artistic events, and not in any way derogatory. Remember I taught you to always respect family, friends and everyone you come in contact with? They are nucleic part of us, one way or the other.

You know that some of the people that you have met and will still meet are without fathers or any father figures. CLEAR THE PASSAGEWAYS ended by admonishing you to be or hold the light for others to see. Of what benefit will it be if we hoard these experiences when we can be fathers to numerous people all over the world? We even make fathers better in their relationship with their sons and daughters as well as their wives because there is no way you can love a child without treating the mother of that child well. And since God has been so kind to us, we should share the blessing with others as that is when we are adjudged wealthy.

Single parenting is so common these days. So many reasons are responsible for that. You will notice that I didn't talk about it in the body of this noteography just because I want us to strive to discourage that. If it is caused by natural occurrence, then it is understandable.

That is not to suggest that people that are in that kind of situation are unfortunate. In fact they are stronger in taking up the challenge to be good parents as I pray that God will see them through it all.

There is no page or even a word in this noteography that is not important. Chew them all. Digest them all and you will glow.

Lest I forget, pass it on to other boys.

I love you son.

'Debayo Coker

BACK TO SCHOOL: ABOUT THE AUTHOR.

𝒟ear son,

How is my granddaughter doing? She should be in the crèche by now since your wife would have gone back to work.

Hey! Hope you have not been calling her MyPD? If you do without getting a written permission from us, then you will be sued for copyright infringement. Don't think MyPD has forgotten how to make representation in the law court yet....LOL.

Call her whatever love code you so choose, MyPD inclusive if you so wish.

My first degree is a Bachelors of Arts in English Language from the Obafemi Awolowo Univeristy, Ile-Ife, Osun state, Nigeria.

I started working in one of the biggest telcos in Africa immediately I finished the mandatory one year National Youth Service to the nation as is statutorily demanded of every graduate of Nigerian descent. I was so fortunate to get a job that was a rarity in the nation at that time.

Many graduates roamed the streets, not because they didn't want to work, but there were no jobs and not so many people had the skills and wherewithal to start something on their own; many people do not know about self-discovery.

About the same time that I got a job, I proceeded to the University of Lagos, Akoka, Lagos, Nigeria to study for a Master's degree in Public and International Affairs.

I spent 6yrs with that telco before I was pushed out because I was foolishly kindhearted by freely giving airtime to people. I learnt life's lessons the hard way, some of which is not to spend what one doesn't earn and how one must not help a friend to cover up his/her debt but only encourage them to be responsible to pay up.

I started Beeni Global Resources (BGR), a company that provides world class consultancy services to corporations regardless of their sizes. We specialize in building, training, staffing and managing the customer service for any company that seeks our services. But son, for many months nothing came as is usual for a new business.

I have always had innate writing skills that I had thought would be my retirement bedrock as I had so many unpublished works of arts, poems, articles, drama and all other literary materials that I was just stockpiling. Almost frustrated due to joblessness, I fell back on them.

Along the way, I got introduced to my two lovely friends. Established writers they are as they have published many books together and individually: Jeff Underwood and Kate Taylor. Those guys that I told you made me have my first insight into snowing. Remember? Those two really brought out the quality of my writing as they sharpened me. Iron sharpens iron. It is always good to move closer to people of like minds.

Writing has been my way of life since then.

In all of those times, I had it at the back of my mind to go back to school, study more and offer myself in building our Ivory Tower.

What do you think about it?

The human mind is fallible. I just remembered that I didn't provide you with an email that you can pass to the public that would like to hear directly from me.

The email address is debayocoker@gmail.com and my twitter handle is adebay_c, I blog via www.pausibility.wordpress.com and my website is www.debayocoker.com. I am open to anything they may want to know.

As for me and you, the conversation continues.

I love you my son.

'Debayo Coker

Made in the USA
Charleston, SC
19 July 2014